The Dare Boys in Vincennes

Stephen Angus Cox

Alpha Editions

This edition published in 2021

ISBN : 9789354545931

Design and Setting By
Alpha Editions
www.alphaedis.com
Email - info@alphaedis.com

As per information held with us this book is in Public Domain. This book is a reproduction of an important historical work. Alpha Editions uses the best technology to reproduce historical work in the same manner it was first published to preserve its original nature. Any marks or number seen are left intentionally to preserve its true form.

Contents

CHAPTER I ASSIGNED TO DUTY. - 1 -
CHAPTER II AN INCIDENT. - 6 -
CHAPTER III A SURPRISE. - 11 -
CHAPTER IV AN ENCOUNTER. - 16 -
CHAPTER V ABOARD THE SLOOP. - 23 -
CHAPTER VI ON THE MARCH. - 29 -
CHAPTER VII ON THE BEACH. - 35 -
CHAPTER VIII THE AMBUSH. - 41 -
CHAPTER IX IN CAMP. - 47 -
CHAPTER X TELCA. - 53 -
CHAPTER XI FOLLOWING THE TRAIL. - 60 -
CHAPTER XII THE NIGHT ATTACK. - 66 -
CHAPTER XIII THE CLIFF DROP. - 73 -
CHAPTER XIV EVADING THE ENEMY. - 79 -
CHAPTER XV UNITED. - 85 -
CHAPTER XVI CONCLUSION. - 90 -

CHAPTER I
ASSIGNED TO DUTY.

In the cool, darkened room of the improvised Patriot Hospital in Charleston, a young man in the uniform of a Continental, read aloud to his much-bandaged friend. The subject of their attention was a long-delayed letter from the invalid's sister, in which she dwelt lightly on the hardships at home, and came forth strongly in praise of her brother's hardy deeds.

"If it wasn't for Dick," said the wounded boy, faintly, but with a smile, "you would imagine I was the Patriot army all by myself."

"It's because you were such a good part of it that you're on your back now," returned Tom Dare with enthusiasm.

In an important engagement near Charleston, Ben Foster had been severely wounded, and for two weeks the Dare Boys, Dick and Tom, feared for their friend's life. That morning, however, the surgeons had relieved their anxiety by promising Ben's recovery, provided he received careful nursing. This good news greatly cheered the two brothers' hearts, for after having passed through so many thrilling occasions in safety, they dreaded the thought of returning to their homes near Philadelphia without their boon companion.

Although the city at this date was in control of the Patriot Army, the British were everywhere about and actively watchful. To go to or communicate with any point beyond the lines was a task fraught with difficulty, and letters were rare events indeed.

Dick Dare, whose latest triumphs under the "Swamp Fox" the reader well remembers, returned at this moment from the commander's quarters and noticed the letter in his comrade's hand.

"News from home?" he inquired, eagerly. "Oh! from your sister, Ben?"

"No," rejoined Tom, bent on arousing his curiosity, for Dick's regard for Ben's sister was well known. "No," he jokingly said, "it's a letter from Fritz Schmockenburg, inviting us to attend an affair at his country estate."

"I'll attend to Fritz's affair later on," Dick began. Then his face grew serious and he added, "When Ben Has gone to sleep, Tom, and you are not wanted here, I want you to run over to the barracks for a few minutes."

"Anything wrong?" inquired Ben.

"Only that I'm off for a little trip, Ben, and I want to give a few final instructions to this good-for-nothing nurse of yours," Dick returned, quietly pushing his brother from the stool on which he was sitting.

"Is that all the general wanted you for?" asked the aggrieved Tom, from his location on the floor. "I was in hopes that he would send you away for a month or two."

"Well, it's very likely to amount to that before I get through." Dick bent close to the bed. "I'm bound for Vincennes, boys, but we are to keep that secret to ourselves."

"Vincennes!" they chorused.

"Why that's way over near the Mississippi river, isn't it?" asked Ben.

"Thereabouts," replied Dick. "I'm sorry I have to go before you are up and around, Ben, but the general has honored me with this commission and I must start at once."

"How about me, cannot I go too?" queried Tom.

"You are to stay here and be good to Ben for a few days and then you are to follow me," answered Dick, dropping his voice to a whisper. "This message that I'm going to carry has got to get through and to insure its delivery a similar message is to be sent and you are to carry it. If one fails the other should succeed. You can follow me as soon as possible, and we may be able to make the last stages of the trip together."

"Sorry I'm out of this," said Ben, "but you can't stop bullets and carry messages at the same time very successfully."

Dick bade him a quiet, but none the less sincere farewell, and hurried over to his quarters to get ready for his trip.

His preparations consisted mainly in a careful examination of the arms he was to carry and his coffee-pot.

He then called to Fritz—the blundering but well-meaning Fritz—with whom the boys had had so many larks, and by a few words startled that individual into incoherent phrases and hurried action. Tom joined him soon afterward and offered his assistance in making ready.

"Hate to hurry you away like this, old man," said Tom, mockingly.

"I am not going to hurry after I start, anyhow," Dick replied. "I'm going to take along an anchor in the form of that ever-slow German, Fritz."

"Fritz," shouted Tom. "Why under the sun is he going with you?"

"To conceal my haste," Dick answered. "If I start out with that symbol of Mercury riding along side of me, no one will suspect that I'm going through an enemy's country, and through unbeaten forests into the heart of the west on an important trip. They will surely think I've gone to that 'affair' on Fritz's estate you were speaking of a short time ago."

"Maybe you're right, Dick," Tom said musingly, "but I suspect that with Fritz along, you will have to travel pretty slowly."

"Nonsense," asserted his brother. "Fritz will go as fast as his horse carries him and won't handicap me in any way."

The boys were soon joined by Fritz with his equipment in his hands. He was bursting with curiosity as to what was in store for him. Dick had merely told him to get ready for a long journey and with the German, Dick's words were law, for he had frequently been saved from dangerous positions by Dick Dare's aid, and held him in the highest esteem.

The three young adventurers gathered about a table at one end of the Dare boys' room and settled themselves to the careful study of a much worn map of the country through which they would have to travel.

"Fritz and I," began Dick, "start tomorrow at daybreak, so as to avoid any more notice than possible, and we are to ride hard after we are outside the British lines, till it gets hot. Then we'll just jog along, either stopping at a farm for our meals or cooking them ourselves, making whatever distance the country permits, and spending the nights, when possible, with Patriot farmers or in the open. One week from today you, Tom, will start for the same point. You are to take Tim Murphy with you. Tim is quick-witted and you ought to be able to follow us rapidly enough to arrive at Fort Pitt about the time we do, for Fritz and I have to blaze the way."

"That sounds like a pleasure excursion, with the British, Tories, and Indians thrown in to add to the interest and keep us from falling asleep."

"Yes, that's the way it sounds," responded Dick, "but remember, young man, that we have to deliver that message exactly one month from today!"

"Never," cried Tom. "Why, Dick, that's impossible. A thousand miles with all those difficulties in front of you! I don't think that even you can do it, Dick."

"It has to be done," said Dick, quietly, "and you've got to try it too, Tom."

"Well, if you can, I can, Dick," answered Tom, spiritedly.

"So it will be a race," cried Dick.

"And may we both win," rejoined his brother, holding out his hand.

"Ver do I come in?" inquired Fritz, for the first time sufficiently collected to speak. "Now dot I am made ready, for once, vy iss it I am going to,—from,—for,—

"You're not," said Tom, severely.

"No," added Dick.

"No!" chimed Fritz.

Then Dick, to help his confused comrade out of his difficulties, explained their proposed journey as clearly as possible to the delight of the soldier, who welcomed an opportunity to distinguish himself in so important a mission, and who was, moreover, greatly pleased at the prospect of a trip with Dick Dare.

While the three young fellows were engrossed in the discussion of their plans, there came to their ears the sound of horses in motion. They were passing under their window and drew the boys' attention outside.

"Our mounts," shouted Dick.

"Our mounds ver?" asked Fritz in a puzzled tone.

"You wait here Fritz and I'll bring them up," said Dick, laughing as he and Tom hurried from the room.

They met the cavalry troopers leading two horses. At the entrance to the barn they made a careful examination of the animals by lamplight.

"A fine pair of horses," said Dick.

"Seem pretty wiry," ventured Tom, and then looking about he added: "Wonder what happened to Fritz?"

"We'll see about that," replied Dick, giving his new possession a final and parting pat. They retraced their steps and reaching the front of the house collided with Fritz. He had just ventured forth in an effort to find out what the others were doing.

"Your horse doesn't care to go up to see you tonight, Fritz," said Dick in an apologetic tone.

"Horse?" echoed Fritz.

"Certainly," replied Tom, having difficulty in restraining his mirth.

"I do't you said it 'mound' vas," protested Fritz.

"That's a 'grave' mistake on your part," answered Tom, as pursued by the laughing Dick and the perplexed Fritz, he fled into the barracks.

"Time to turn in, I guess, as long as Fritz and I have to be up so early in the morning," Dick yawned.

So the three youths upon whom during the next few weeks so much was to depend, rolled themselves up in their blankets and with a muffled "Good night," closed their eyes for the last time together for many a night.

CHAPTER II
AN INCIDENT.

"Getting warm, isn't it" commented Dare about eleven o'clock the morning of their first day on the road.

"Dot's right, py jimminy," panted Fritz, mopping the perspiration from his red face. "But we fooled those Red-goats that time, eh Dick?"

"I'm not so sure," Dick replied gravely. "I'm very much afraid they knew that everything wasn't as it should be, and that they will suspect our mission. And if they do, we are going to have trouble before we arrive at Vincennes."

Dick was referring to the incident of their passing the British lines early that morning. One of the guards was inclined to be suspicious. Dick's seeming frank explanation but more particularly Fritz's innocent and guileless manner, however, had temporarily, at least, won the day.

"Dot's an unbolite feller up the road, Dick," muttered the German boy, pointing ahead. "See him vaving his arms and hands at a young frauline like he vas her jailor."

Dick shaded his eyes with his hand and surveyed the couple to whom Fritz had called his attention. The man was unquestionably threatening his companion with violence, and the girl, although she made no effort to escape, glanced back frequently as if looking about her for assistance.

"Come on, let's investigate," cried Dick, putting spurs to his horse. Fritz followed closely, and the pair soon overtook the two pedestrians whom they had observed. As they rode up, the man, who was evidently a young southerner, seized his companion by the wrist, at which she cried out.

"That strikes me as very poor courtesy," shouted Dick, reining up, "and is most surprising to see in a man of this state!"

"State," snapped the other, still retaining his hold on the girl, who looked as if she might be his sister, as the boys soon discovered she was. "To all but rebels this is a loyal colony of His Majesty, King George."

"Rebels is a hard word," replied Dick, "and, moreover, my friend and I shall be indebted to you if you will immediately release the lady, who doesn't appear to be greatly flattered with your attentions."

"Yah," chorused Fritz. "So are we."

"You don't seem to lack admirers," drawled the southerner, turning to his sister. Then, his rage overcoming him, "You little rebel spy!" he hissed.

The girl paled, and at this added insult Dick leaped to the ground and advanced on the troublesome one. Grasping him by the collar and giving him a vigorous push in the proper direction, Dick sent the young Loyalist sprawling in a ditch.

"Ha, ha!" shouted Fritz, "my turn next."

"It will be both of your turns next," yelled their new acquaintance, who had promptly recovered his feet, and was retiring down the road in discomfort, evidently feeling sure that retreat was the safest in the face of such odds.

"Oh," cried the girl, "now I've drawn you into trouble, haven't I?"

"Not that I can notice," replied Dick, with quiet indifference. "I trust that we have been of service to you and haven't interfered where we shouldn't have."

"I can't thank you enough for getting rid of him just at this moment," she replied. "As he said, I'm a Patriot, and he was trying to force some important information from me regarding the forces in Charleston."

"My name is Dare, miss, and this is Fritz Schmockenburg, both of Capt. Morgan's company."

The girl nodded brightly at Fritz, who was overwhelmed by the suddenness with which he was thrown into a lady's company. "My brother is very influential in the King's army," she said, "and now I'd advise you to hurry along if you expect to avoid any further trouble with him."

At that moment Dick thought he distinguished the dull sound of hoofbeats coming from the direction in which the young Tory had retreated.

"Guess you're right," replied Dick, "but if we go on, what will happen to you?"

"My house is around the bend in the road," the girl answered quickly, "I'll cut through these woods and be safe in two minutes. But you must hurry, for he won't come back alone."

"Good-bye and good luck," cried Dick as he watched her spring lightly over the stone wall at the side of the road. "All aboard, Fritz, I reckon they're after us," and suiting action to the word, Dick vaulted into his saddle and started away at a gallop.

The pursuing Redcoats could be seen plainly now, urging their horses on in the hopes of overtaking the young patriots before they had gathered speed. The two groups fairly flew along the dusty highway, and Dick, bending low over his saddle, saw the pursuers drawing their pistols.

"Bend down, Fritz," he shouted, "but don't try to return their fire."

Even as he spoke there was the sound of discharged firearms.

"Ach, I'm a dead one alreaty," hollered Fritz, and before Dick could reply or offer aid, the German boy clutched madly at his horse's mane and then rolled in a heap in the dust of the road. His fall was greeted with yells from the soldiers, who quickly approaching soon surrounded his prostrate form and abandoned any further pursuit of Dick.

"Just what Tom said," muttered Dick, as after a hard gallop he slowed down his panting horse and wiped the dust from his eyes. "Here, on the first day out, Fritz is captured and probably wounded seriously, and I can't go on my mission till I find out how he is and what I can do for him."

Dick rode slowly onward for half a mile more, and then turned off in the bed of a stream which crossed the road at this point. The brook rapidly narrowed to a rushing little fall, and here, completely away from sight or sound of travellers along the road, he jumped from his tired horse, permitted him a refreshing drink at the brook, and, after hobbling him securely, turned his attention toward preparing a meal for one.

Dick moistened a handful of flour with water, kneaded it with his fingers into a clinging dough, and set it aside while he built his fire. He was particular to pick out dry pieces of moss and hard twigs, for smoke was a thing to be avoided, and the hard woods burn freest.

Having gradually increased the size of his fuel and consequently the blaze, until he judged it hot enough, Dick drew his hunting knife, cut two pieces of bacon from his precious store, and laid them in the pan on the coals. The dough he now rolled into flat round cakes and placed in the pan with the bacon to fry. Carefully turning the cakes and bacon from time to time with the flat of his knife, he prepared a meal fit for a king, but destined to be eaten by an enemy of all kings.

Dick fretted and fumed all that afternoon, and toward dusk ventured out from his retreat and rode slowly back in the direction of the British camps, whose exact whereabouts he had to determine. At the top of a slight rise he saw in the distance the glow of the soldiers' camp-fire, and making his horse fast to a tree, some distance from the road, he proceeded carefully on foot toward the sentinel lines and the British encampment.

Half way up to the camp he dropped flat on the ground and waited for the nearest outpost to come to the end of his stretch, exchange a word with his neighbor, and turn back. Then Dick crawled between the two while their backs were turned, and was safely inside the lines. But where was Fritz? And how badly was he wounded? Could he have been killed?

Dick, after considerable reconnoitering, located a stout log house in front of which a sentry strolling was talking to his nearby companions around a fire. Dick was near enough to hear plainly all that was said.

"The old Dutchman snores," laughed the sentinel.

"Hurray," thought Dick, "that means Fritz and then he can't be very seriously wounded."

Dick crept up behind the hut, which was built of stout logs, and discovered with joy that there was a small barred window. Through this he lightly threw a small stone to attract the prisoner's attention.

"Get oud," yelled Fritz, who was surprised from his sleep by the missle.

"Wait till I come in," said his guard, from the other side of the house. "Quit your Dutch dreams and prepare to go on to the next world, cause you're due to take that trip tomorrow, sure."

"Not if I know it," thought Dick.

Then when things had quieted down again, he called to Fritz softly through the window. The German boy got up from the couch on which he was lying and looked out cautiously. He almost shouted when he distinguished his friend in the semi-darkness.

"Are you badly hurt, Fritz?" asked Dick anxiously.

"Nein," was the answer, "dot fool saddle slipped the horse off and me and mine horse went mit it the dust into."

"Good," ejaculated Dick, "I'm glad it's no worse. Now how about getting out?"

"Dere iss a chimney big enough," said Fritz, "and the door is only barred on the other side, but there is a soldier there."

"The chimney, then," said Dick, "for we can't get past the guard at the door. Why haven't you escaped before this?"

"Vell, I fell asleep ven they put me in here, and you voke me up just now," confessed Fritz, sheepishly.

"Up the chimney now, quick," ordered Dick, "and be quiet, too."

Fritz disappeared, and after quite an interval Dick saw his stout comrade laboriously climbing over the top of the structure. But Dick wasn't alone in this strange sight. One of the soldiers saw him too, and, yelling out the alarm, sprang for his gun just as Fritz jumped to the ground. Dick leading, both started running through the woods.

The two fugitives made a detour through the underbrush, tearing their clothes and making noise enough to guide the pursuing Red-coats. Dick and Fritz turned sharply to the left, stepping quietly for a few paces, and found themselves in the opening, before the very prison Fritz had so recently deserted, while the chase streamed by in the darkened woods, and the cries of the soldiers roused the neighboring fire-groups to action.

"Into the hut," whispered Dick. "It's our only chance. The woods are alive with troops and we'd be caught in no time."

"But I just got oud," objected Fritz. "And I don't——"

"In you go," said Dick, giving him a push, and following the hurried and astonished boy, he closed the door after them and stepped to the window.

"They have got us safe enough, if they only knew it," thought Dick. He turned to Fritz. "They'll come back here soon to see how you climbed out. We've got to hide somewhere. Quick, they're coming now! Under that straw in the corner, Fritz. I'll take care of myself. Way under, now!"

CHAPTER III
A SURPRISE.

Two days before the week succeeding the departure of Dick and his comrade had elapsed, Tom and Tim made their preparations to start after them. Ben had progressed nicely and was able to sit up and take an interest in life once more. After a long consultation with the commander the boys had arranged to make the first part of the trip by water. This in order to avoid the suspicion that they were following Dick and thus prevent the real importance of their mission from being discovered.

Toward evening of the day of their departure, Tim Murphy, overflowing with true Irish wit and humor, and full of expectations of an exciting trip with Tom Dare, climbed gaily aboard the long, low-built schooner that was to convey them up the coast to the Chesapeake.

"Sure, and it's welcome ye are to my private yacht, Tom," he called over the side to his companion. "Come aboard and join me party of friends who are thinkin' of cruisin' about for a few weeks at me expense."

"There will be a murder at your expense when the captain sees those muddy marks on his white deck," replied Tom. "She is a beauty though, isn't she?" he continued, gazing critically over the craft's lines and rigging.

"That she is," agreed Tim.

"Avast, you land-lubber," bellowed a voice from the fore-deck.

"Told you so," whispered Tom.

"What did I do?" queried Tim, staring about to discover the cause of the trouble.

"Oh, probably the gentleman who just spoke recognized you," laughed Tom.

"Ow!" yelled Tim, for at that moment a can of varnish which one of the sailors had been lowering from the masthead, reached Tim, and tilting slightly, covered his face with the sticky fluid.

"I'll be after haulin' ye to the gineral," shouted the outraged Tim. "Insultin' a special soldier on special duty is a serious offince."

"You look like a very special soldier," Tom managed to say between his bursts of laughter.

The appearance on the deck of the captain saved Tim from further disgrace, and after extending a hearty welcome to Tom and his offended companion, he led the two boys below and showed them their bunks. Tim hurriedly got rid of the varnish and joined Tom in the captain's cabin.

"We're all sailors together when we are on board, boys," began their new host. "The general has told me that you know something of sailing, and a little of navigating," turning to Tom, "so I'll ask you to assist the mate in standing watch. Perhaps as long as you are more or less of an amateur it will help you to have Tim with you on your watch. We sail at nine tonight, dropping down with the tide, and your turn won't come until tomorrow morning, so turn in, boys, and get in a good night's rest before the work begins."

The two new members of the crew found themselves ready for their bunks when the time came, and slept peacefully until early morning, when Tom was awakened by an unearthly shouting. Sitting up quietly in his bunk he rapped his head sharply against the bottom of the upper bunk, and before he had recovered his wits he was pounced upon by three sailors.

More quickly than it can be described he was bound and trussed like a fowl, and carried forward along the decks. Here he was promptly lowered into the dark hold, and found lying beside him the unfortunate Tim, gagged to prevent his shouts from disturbing the mutineers, together with the mate and captain in the same plight with himself.

Meanwhile the hatch had been battened down and nothing broke the stillness of the hold save the swish of the waves outside and the uneven breathing of his companions.

After considerable wriggling, Tom was able to reach Tim's gag with his hands and finally worked it loose.

"Now keep quiet," cautioned Tom, "or you'll have that pack of traitors back at us. Tell me what happened to you and what the meaning of this pretty affair is."

"You know as well as I do," returned the injured Tim. "I woke up with half the bloody wretches jumping on me and tying ropes all over me, so I just hollered and here I am."

"The captain and mate are hurt," Tom said. "If you will turn over on your side so I can reach your wrists, perhaps the knots will loosen up, and we can get the use of our limbs again. Then we'll look for some water to bring the captain around with."

The knots were more trouble than Tom had expected, and by the time Tim was free, the captain and mate showed signs of returning consciousness. Tim speedily released his friend, and together they loosed the two prisoners' bonds and chafed their wrists to restore circulation.

A hasty tour of the hold revealed to Tom a half dozen water casks and a canvas bucket in which he drew some of the cool liquid, and returned to the side of the captain and his fellow sufferer. The water sprinkled on them soon stirred the two men into renewed life, and after gazing about for a few moments they both broke forth into imprecations against their faithless crew.

"Unlucky day that I ever shipped that pack of robbers," muttered the captain. "A lot of Portuguese and Tories, probably well paid by the enemies of Liberty, turning against their captain on the high seas. They'll hang to the yard arm for this or I never saw a ship before."

"Guess we'll have quite a long day's work hanging all of them, won't we?" asked Tom. "Seems to me that we are more apt to be those hanging decorations ourselves unless we can get out of their way before long."

"They'll be too busy tending to business for a while," answered the mate. "From the sound of the water alongside, I judge there has blown up a pretty stiff breeze, and as far as I know, none of those villains knows any too much about handling a ship."

"Hope they know enough to keep her right side up," said Tom, "otherwise we'll be likely to gather no moss till we reach bottom."

"If they don't come down before night," the captain continued, "we ought to be able to get into the little galley under my cabin, and get the arms that we have on board. I don't think they are very well equipped with either guns or powder, though there's plenty of both on board. If they only give us time we'll have the best of it yet, and then—" The captain drifted on half to himself going over all the dire punishments the unruly crew might expect should he once get them into his power.

The day wore on without any visits from the men ashore, and it was well toward dusk before the four prisoners heard the hatch above them being removed.

"If they find us with the ropes all off, they'll probably tie us up tighter than ever," said Tom in a hurried whisper.

"Back to the stern part of this old hole," grunted the captain. "We can hide there for a few minutes, and I may be able to get the trap open into the musket room. We ought to be able to stand them off with clubbed guns until night, and then we'll make a try for the powder and shot."

The hatch had in the meantime been removed, and in the square above Tom could see the fast darkening sky, with two heads peering down into the darkness below.

"Can't see the old rats, can you?" said one.

"Have to get a lantern and investigate," answered the other. "Hey, Jack pass us a light, and come along below. Going to pay a visit to the captain and his good friends."

"Let's give them a warm reception," whispered Tom. "We four can easily surprise the three of them, and before they can get any help from above, we can get away, and climb into your store-house, captain."

"Go ahead," replied the captain, only too glad of the chance to settle scores with some of his rebel crew.

As the three sailors slowly descended the ladder, the first one carrying the lantern, our four friends stole softly nearer to the limited circle of light cast by the lantern's flickering rays.

The foremost sailor had just reached the bottom, when with a shout, Tim sprang for the man highest up, and, catching him by the ankles, threw him heavily from the ladder. The other two, taken by surprise at this unexpected assault from the men they had supposed to be bound, made very little trouble for the three Patriots, and were soon rolled up in the same ropes that their victims had recently escaped from.

The mutineers overhead hearing the scuffle in the hold, crowded about the hatchway, shouting questions to their comrades.

"Come down and see what's the matter," yelled the captain. "There's room for all of you in the same place your friends are stowed."

"We'll keep up the talk," interposed Tom quietly, "while you get the trap open into the gun room."

The captain hurried off into the darkness, while Tim, the mate and Tom kept up a running fire of comment with the sailors overhead.

"Come along and jine the bunch of us," yelled Tim, in his best Celtic. "We're after holding a small reception in our private quarters."

No response to his sally came from the hatch, and Tom' noticed the gradual addition of a number of sailors with lanterns about the opening.

"Hope there's enough of them left from this little tea-party to trim ship," said the mate, who had undertaken the duty of watching their three prisoners.

"Guess they'll take good care of their own skins," Tom replied. "Even if they don't show much regard for ours."

"Your friends is havin' a foine time," shouted Tim, whom no situation could frighten, "and we'll all be glad to see yez with us if you'll only accipt our invitation."

"You'd better be careful or they will be with us altogether too soon," interposed Tom.

"Right you are," the mate continued. "They won't stay away from us after they find we are unarmed for very long."

The group on deck had evidently reached some conclusion at this minute for a pair of legs followed by a long blue jacketed body appeared on the upper rungs of the ladder and the first of the sailors began a careful descent. He carried a long dirk in his belt, and the three on guard shouted to the captain that they would have to join him soon.

"Hold up a minute and I'll be ready for you," the captain replied. "Just a couple of shakes, and we'll be all right."

The three Patriots retreated into the darkness of the afterhold, and the first invader jumped to the bottom of the ladder, where he was speedily joined by half a dozen of his companions.

"Let us out of this," cried the captive sailors, who had been roped up by the boys. "Let us have a whack at them too."

"What's in these kegs?" whispered Tom to the mate, pointing to a small round object he had fallen over.

"Powder," replied the mate. "Why?"

Quick as a flash, Tom ran his fingers around the keg, until he found the plug. Working this loose a fine stream of black powder ran out and formed a little mound beside the keg. Tom hastily added more to this and spread it out in a thin line running toward the captain.

Tim, grasping his idea, helped all he could to lengthen the thin trail of powder, and they soon had a fuse of considerable length running from the keg to the trap in the gun room.

The mutineers were now starting toward the four prisoners, and as they approached to within a dozen yards of the keg, Tom cried out:

"Keep back or we'll send this old boat to the bottom. Another step and I'll touch off these powder kegs in front of you!"

CHAPTER IV
AN ENCOUNTER.

After seeing Fritz scramble under the heap of straw in the corner of the hut, Dick's eyes roamed about the enclosure in search of a place to conceal himself. He could hear the Redcoats returning to the clearing after their fruitless pursuit of the two boys, and he knew that there was no time to waste before getting out of sight.

Suddenly he hit upon the best remaining hiding place, an old grain chest in the corner, and quickly raising the lid he climbed inside and lowered it. For awhile all was silent, and just as Dick had decided that it would be wise to get out of his new residence and look about, he heard the indistinct murmur of voices, and heavy footsteps sounded on the cabin floor.

"The rebel got out through the chimney," said the first voice.

"Go along. He was too fat to get out of there," said the second.

"Oh, I saw him, as I told you," repeated the first, "and if you hadn't been asleep on your job you'd have seen him, too."

"Well, I don't care how he got out. So long as he's gone we can't help it," the disgruntled trooper replied. "For one, I'm glad he's out of this cozy box. I'm going to camp in here myself."

"Ought to be room for four or five of us, I guess," another Redcoat chimed in. "And there's a nice stack of straw for my bed."

"Poor Fritz," thought Dick. "Caught again. Well, if I'm able to get out of this I may be able to help him again. I'm afraid coming back here was a bad plan the way things are working out."

A dispute had arisen, however, amongst the soldiers as to who was entitled to the heap of straw, and after some scuffling and much wordy war, they agreed to leave the straw where it was, and all slept on their blankets.

"Hope Fritz doesn't get up and thank them for leaving him alone," Dick thought. "And now, with this pleasant little addition to our party, however are we going to get away?"

The soldiers were soon rolled up in their coverings, and despite the excitement of their recent chase, they quickly dropped off to sleep, as Dick could tell from the constantly growing volume of snores.

After allowing all the time he felt he could to let his unwitting captors drift soundly into the land of dreams, Dick carefully raised the cover of his bin, and stuck his head out to look around. The fires outside had died down, and the light inside was very scarce indeed.

Suddenly Dick heard a rustle from the straw pile and he realized that Fritz had about exhausted his ability to keep motionless. Dick quietly raised himself over the side of the box, and stepping cautiously over two sleeping Redcoats, crept to the hiding place of Fritz. How to uncover his friend without making a noise was a problem, but proceeding with great care and skill, he gradually removed part of the straw from Fritz, and whispering to him to be perfectly quiet till he finished, Dick gradually had the German boy free of all trouble, and together they tiptoed to the door of the hut.

Directly outside, however, some more of the soldiers were sleeping, and both Dick and Fritz in their eagerness to get away from their surroundings stumbled over one of the sleeping forms and immediately aroused the enemy to a knowledge of their presence.

The yells of the startled Redcoats filled the woods, and with Fritz dashing madly after the fleeing Dick, the two quickly reached the outskirts of the camp.

"I see the horses," panted Dick. "We must try to get yours."

"Yah. Get me a horse," answered Fritz, between breaths. "Myself won't carry much more."

Although the soldiers were heard not a great distance back, Dick dashed to the tether rope and slashed it with his knife. At that moment the trooper guarding the horses sprang upon him, but Fritz had presence of mind enough left to grab him about the waist, and the two rolled on the ground locked in each others arms. Fritz's horse was on the end of the line, and grasping the halter to secure him, Dick shouted and slapped at the nearest trooper's horses to stampede them. He was more successful than he had hoped and the frightened animals turned and galloped off in all directions, many of them heading for the pursuing Redcoats.

The confusion that resulted was a great help to the two patriots, and as Fritz had freed himself from the clutches of the soldier he had been fighting with, the two boys made their escape in the darkness and soon picked up Dick's horse, at some little distance from the camp.

"I'm more than thankful to be out of that," said Dick, earnestly, when they had galloped a little way along the road.

"But vere do we sleep?" asked Fritz. "For myself this is a hard day."

"Sleep," echoed Dick, "we won't get any of that before noon-day, I guess. We've got to keep moving while the darkness helps us."

They had now covered a mile or more along the road, and Fritz was drooping in his saddle from exhaustion, when, without warning, from the road ahead a figure cried, "Halt!"

The command was accompanied by the ominous click of a musket hammer being raised, and as Dick pulled at the bridle of Fritz's horse and attempted to wheel them both, he felt himself grasped by strong hands. Despite his efforts he was quickly pulled from his mount.

Fritz was soon placed beside him, and the leader, after gruffly cautioning the boys to be quiet, gave the order to march, and the band with its prisoners in their midst moved on in the direction which the boys had been following. Evidently they had ridden into their ranks before discovering the presence of anyone else, and had fallen easy victims into their hands.

It was still some time before day, and the tired boys had great difficulty in keeping up to the rapid strides of their captors.

Finally, after what seemed an age to Fritz, the dark turned into a dull grey and Dick, peering at the men about him, suddenly emitted a shout that brought the men about him threateningly.

"They're our men, Fritz! Hurray!" he cried. "We're all right, after all!"

"Give us back our horse," grumbled Fritz, provoked at having walked when he might have ridden.

"Boys, this is a mistake," explained Dick. "We're Patriots on a special mission, and we trust you'll help us make up this needless loss of time."

"Fine Patriots you would make," answered one of the band. "You're a couple of Tory spies and you can't fool your Uncle Henry by any such story as that."

"You're wrong," cried Dick. "You're dead wrong. Isn't there any of you here that know us? This is Fritz Schmockenberg, of Captain Morgan's company. I'm Dick Dare," he explained modestly.

"Ha, ha," laughed one of the men. "So you're Dick Dare, are you? Well, let me tell you, my young friend, that Dick Dare is in Charleston, and we left him there only yesterday."

"That's what everybody is supposed to think," replied Dick. "We left there secretly."

"That don't go with us," said the leader, coming forward. "You fellows are from the British force which is quartered a space back along the road, and I'm afraid that under the usual rules of war, you will have to pay the penalty that is usually dealt out to spies."

"For why didn't we stay vere ve vass," lamented Fritz. "Dot straw vas so comfortable."

"Where were you?" questioned the Patriot captain.

"In dot Redgoat hut," answered Fritz, without thinking of the effect such a statement would have.

"Just what I thought," cried the Patriot, exultingly. "What have you got to say to that?" turning to Dick.

"What he says is true," answered Dick. "We just escaped from the hands of the British, and thought we had run into another of their parties when you took us in charge."

"Well, we don't string up prisoners without a chance to explain themselves," returned the leader, "but I can't say as I see much hope for you fellows. You admit coming from the enemy's camp, and don't explain matters till you think up this fool story about being Patriots. I kind of think you are British spies and in these times we can't afford to be taking many chances."

"You are making an awful mistake," answered Dick. "If we could only be taken before one of your commanders, I'm sure they would know me. I'm afraid I can't explain anything any more fully." Dick kept in mind the secrecy of his instructions, and did not feel that he could betray his trust under any circumstances.

The company resumed their march and a few of the officers withdrew and entered into an earnest discussion. They were one of the bands of local Patriots who roamed about the country and joined whatever organized movement was afoot in their vicinity. They were a great thorn in the side of the British, but due to their irresponsibility and lack of order, were not generally sought after by the Patriot armies.

After marching some distance along the road, the men turned off to one side, crossed a few fields, and entered a patch of woods to cook breakfast and rest after their tiring march. The two boys shared in the breakfast and exchanged a few comments with each other, but talking to the men who were about them was forbidden.

With their simple repast out of the way the men lay back and took their ease preparatory to taking up their tramp again. The leaders now approached Dick and Fritz and proceeded to question them about the British force they had just left.

"How many men were there in the Redcoats' camp?" asked the captain.

"About two hundred, I should think," said Dick.

"As long as you are making your last statements on this earth, you may as well stick to the truth," commented the second in command, brutally.

"Bud," Fritz cried, "we would rather stick to the earth." The men could not refrain from laughing at his unintentional joke.

"If you hang us as spies," Dick said, boldly, "you will regret it before long. As soon as the general hears of your horrible mistake I imagine you will have to pay the penalty for your haste."

"That's our lookout, young man," returned the leader. "We can't see anything else to do under the circumstances. You admit having come from the British camp, and didn't declare yourselves when we caught you, so I guess your story won't stand in the face of the evidence against you."

Things looked very black to the two boys at that moment, and there passed before the minds of each all of the incidents in their exciting young lives. Meanwhile the soldiers prepared two ropes to place about their necks, and after asking for any last requests they had to make, led the boys to a strong tree and threw the ends of the ropes over the lower branches.

The two youths had borne themselves bravely through this ordeal and were prepared to go to the end, whatever it might be, in a suitable manner, although Fritz was nearly in tears at the thought of what their finish must be.

"I can't forgive myself for bringing you into this, Fritz," said Dick, brokenly.

"Dot's all right," said Fritz, "mapy der ropes vill preak."

Before Dick could reply to the German's humorous remark and forlorn hope, a brisk volley was fired from around a bend in the road, and the Patriot outposts ran hurriedly toward the shelter of the trees, one of them falling before he had gone more than a few paces, badly wounded by the first discharge.

The men quickly abandoned Dick and Fritz, and grasping their guns, ran crouching to the nearest stone wall in front of them.

"It's the British!" cried one of the pickets.

"Come on, men, and we'll give a good account of ourselves," shouted the captain. "Keep behind the walls and they can't touch us."

He and the other leaders rushed across the field toward the oncoming British. The latter swept around the bend in the road in regular formation and fired a volley with telling effect at the Patriot band. The leaders, more impetuous than the men, suffered severely, and all of them dropped either dead or wounded. The men, however, kept on and without further loss gained the shelter of the stone wall. But without their leaders the defence gradually weakened and the men began to drop back and take refuge behind the second wall. The boys had been onlookers up to this point, but the defeat of the Patriots was too much for their enthusiasm and with the ropes still hanging, unheeded about their necks and trailing out behind, the two youths leaped to the front and snatching up guns from the dead soldiers, shouted to the demoralized and scattering members of the band.

"Come on, men!" Dick cried. "Don't let them get the best of us now! A few more volleys and we'll have them on the run."

"Yah, yah, yah!" chorused Fritz, following Dick and brandishing the musket above his head. He and Dick reached the second stone wall behind which the men were seeking shelter.

The English troopers were holding the first wall and were contemplating a charge across the field to drive the Patriots from their position when Dick took charge.

"Fritz!" he cried, above the roar of the battle. "Take a dozen of these fellows around and through the woods and take the British on the flank!"

"Dot's it!" answered Fritz, catching his friend's idea quickly. "We'll did it."

Dick motioned a handful of the men apart and told them to follow Fritz if they hoped to win out that day and save their liberty. Dick Dare's commanding tone and natural leadership inspired the men with new life, and the few men left with him redoubled their efforts to cover the departure of their comrades and hold the Redcoats off. Their firing, however, was growing more and more infrequent, and the English troops were beginning to climb over the stone wall to charge across the field when Fritz and his men broke out of the woods and yelling like a hundred Indians charged upon the rear of the British.

"Now's the time, boys," called Dick, leaping onto the fence in front of them. "We'll finish the argument now."

"NOW IS THE TIME", CALLED DICK.

The band jumped up with a cheer and followed Dick's lead, rushed madly over the open ground and took the startled enemy off their guard. The combined onslaught of the two bands was more than the British could withstand. After a few minutes of hand-to-hand conflict the English broke and fled headlong for the road. The exulting Patriots followed them for some distance, making several prisoners, and at last, wearied with the long encounter and the pursuit, they dropped back and collected at the scene of the opening of the fight. They had lost half a dozen men and several of the others were wounded, but the victory was complete and amongst their prisoners were two of the Redcoat officers.

The boys came back among the last and the sight of the two brought cheers from the victors. The boys received these quietly and when the shouting was over, Dick stepped forward and spoke to them.

"Let this be a lesson to you, friends," he said soberly. "My friend Fritz and I were nearly murdered by you without proper trial and on entirely insufficient evidence. I think that the little parts that we have played in this combat have proved our loyalty to the cause of liberty, and both Fritz and I hope that any future prisoners will receive better treatment until they are proven guilty."

The men took Dick's little talk to heart and when, after a long rest and a meal the boys left the band, they both felt that any other Patriots who were encountered by this particular band would receive the best of treatment.

CHAPTER V
ABOARD THE SLOOP.

The captain of the sloop had managed to get the door into his gun-room open just in time, for the mate, Tim and Tom had barely scrambled through when the sailors broke toward them in a rush. The captain slammed down the hatch and they all jumped on top, holding it in place while he clamped it fast.

"I doubt if they will find the other entrance," the captain said. "The crew never knew of this place and they won't be likely to disturb us from the other side."

"I guess they will be satisfied to have us boxed up here," said Dick.

"And as far as I kin see it's satisfied they might be," returned Tim. "How should you figger we are goin' to git out av the place?"

"We'll wait around till it grows dark outside," replied the captain, in an undertone, "and then we'll try to gain the after deck and clear those villains off. Then we will have the ship in our control, so that, with proper luck we'll run in near shore and drive the crew off the decks altogether. The four of us can handle this craft till we make a port and then we'll be able to ship a loyal crew and not a parcel of thieves."

"Fine!" ejaculated Tim. "But why be waiting in this stuffy old box whin we might be lords of the ship by runnin' the monkeys into the ocean?"

"No use taking chances, Tim," replied Tom. "If they get us again we won't make such an easy get away, you can bet."

"That's right," the captain commented. "They'd finish us this time if they could get their hands on us. We have got to win or pay the penalty tonight."

These adverse opinions served to quiet Tim's ardor, and he sat about with the rest waiting for night to throw its blanket of darkness over the scene, and for the rebellious crew to quiet down for the night.

As the time wore on, the Patriots could hear the dull tramping of the mutineers in the cabin next to them, and the muffled sound of voices sifted through the heavy oak partitions. The captain and Tom busied themselves with the muskets and ammunition, and after selecting four guns, a dirk and a cutlass for each of the party, did what they could to put the remaining arms out of commission.

The sounds from the cabin had ceased now, and the four sat impatiently awaiting the moment when they could make their great dash for liberty. Gradually it grew quiet and when they decided that it was safe to venture through the cabin to the after-deck, they quietly loosened the trap and peered into the dimly lit cabin.

The recumbent figures of half a dozen mutineers were seen by the aid of the smoky swinging lamp. Judging from the sounds of heavy breathing, this particular party of sailors were fast asleep. The captain, Tim, the mate and Tom crawled carefully through the opened trap, pushed it closed after them and tip-toed for the short ladder leading to the deck.

The swinging doors at the top of the ladder banged at this moment and the four crouched down, fearing that they would have to start their battle then and there, and under most unfavorable circumstances. One of the men muttered, rolled over and resumed his heavy breathing and the danger was over for a moment.

Following the captain, the three Patriots ascended the steps, pushed the door open and with a rush made for the man at the wheel. Not expecting an attack from this quarter, he was overcome with slight effort, and while Tim and the captain carried him to the ladder leading to the main deck, the mate took charge of the wheel and Tom made fast the cabin doors through which they had just emerged.

"What's going on up there?" came a voice from the lower deck. "Everything all right, eh?"

"Sure, foine as silk," shouted Tim.

"Whot's that?" the sailor queried, noticing the commotion about the wheel.

"Your captain, you scoundrel!" that individual replied. "And now I guess we have got you fellows where you belong. The first man that starts for this deck gets what you all deserve."

"Tim!" called Tom. "You and the mate take the starboard ladder, and I'll try the port. Don't let 'em get within twenty feet of you. And don't be afraid to use those muskets. That's what we've toted 'em up here for."

"That's it," replied Tim. "There'll be none of the crowd gets past us this night."

"Aye, aye," chimed in the mate. "We'll do our part and you just holler if you want any help."

"Oh, I'll be all right," answered Tom confidently. "I don't think those fellows are armed and I guess these guns won't appeal to them very favorably."

"Hard-a-lea!" yelled the captain. "I'm going to try to hold her on the other tack and see if we don't fetch up somewhere near the shore."

"Let her go," responded Tom. "Guess the nearer that we get to land the better it will be for us."

"We can't do much toward working the ship," the captain said, "but I don't see why we can't hold her in the right direction as long as we have control of the wheel and the mainsail."

"Which we have," put in Tim.

"Yes, just at present," responded the mate, at his side. "But there's no telling for how long."

"Ahoy, on deck!" came a cry from the cabin. "What's all this? Let us out, you lubbers!"

"Can't be done, me boys," called out Tim. "We have quite enough av us here now."

This was followed by muffled blows on the cabin doors, but the heavy oak and the iron bar withstood all attempts to force it, and after further ineffectual efforts the group within abandoned their efforts and sought escape in other directions.

Tom could now distinguish the men on the lower deck quite plainly, and in a minute or two, one of them came aft toward him.

"You fellows might as well give in now as ever," said the sailor. "We will get you anyhow, and it will go hard with you if we have any trouble with you."

"Well, if you leave it to us," answered Tom, "we prefer to be gotten later, and in the meantime, let me warn you that the next man that comes within twenty feet of these ladders gets what you all deserve."

"That's fine talk, young fellow, but—" and just then the sailor drew back his arm, hurled something violently at Tom and sprang back before Tom could recover from his surprise.

A shining streak went past him and buried itself for an inch in the rail.

"It's a knife," called out the captain. "You want to be a little more careful and not let them get near enough again."

"You bet I will," replied Tom, startled by his narrow escape.

There was a moment's lull in the excitement, and then a crash resounded from directly below Tim's feet.

"Ouch!" yelled the Irish boy, and discharged his musket wildly into the darkness.

"That was only a bucket of paint," said Tom. "Don't be so free with your bullets."

"Faith, an' I thought it was all killed we were," responded Tim, rather ashamed of his sudden alarm.

"Not yet," replied the mate, with a grim attempt at humor.

"Cheer up," said Tom, in the same strain. "The worst is yet to come."

It was evident to the four on the after deck that the mutineers were as yet without guns, for they would have picked off the boys where they stood against the sky line, had they been able.

But the battle was not won yet, in fact it had hardly begun. While the boys and the mate were gazing through the darkness at the knot of men near the forecastle, three sailors suddenly dashed from behind the main mast, and rushed for Tim's position near the ladder. He and the mate fired in unison at them, and evidently wounded one of their number, for with a howl of pain from the foremost, the three scuttled back toward the bow.

"That's good, Tim," called Tom. "We'll hold 'em all right, eh?"

"Don't want 'em near enough to hold," replied Tim.

"That's painful," commented the mate, at Tim's attempted jest.

"Get back there!" shouted Tom, catching sight of a dark form stealing along the bulwarks.

But instead of getting back, the man jumped from the foot of Tom's ladder, and grasped the upper steps. Tom discharged the musket almost in the fellow's face, and with a groan he fell back on the deck. His comrades, however, now swarmed about the base of the ladder, and Tom, grasping his gun by the barrel, swung it with all his force on the head of the foremost sailor.

The man following, however, succeeded in getting a foothold on the upper deck, and with an upraised dirk, drove Tom back from the ladder. Tom swung at him with the clubbed musket, knocked the dirk out of his upraised hand, and in another second was locked with him in hand to hand conflict.

"Tim!" yelled Tom.

"Coming!" answered Tim, and leaving the mate to guard their side, where the mutineers had been driven back, he rushed around the cabin to the aid of his friend.

He was just in time. Tom and his opponent were rolling on the deck, each endeavoring to put the other out of the fight, and two more sailors were about to step upon the deck from the ladder.

Leaving Tom to take care of himself, Tim attacked the ascending sailors. With a rush and wild shouts, he banged the foremost over the head and sent him crashing down upon the others of the group. Then firing his musket at the crowd, he completed their route, and the whole party fled to the shelter of the forecastle.

"And now, where are ye, Tom?" he called.

"Here," Tom replied, coming from behind the cabin. "If I hadn't hit that fellow on the arm before he closed with me, and knocked his dirk out of his grasp, he might have put me out of the way."

"Where did ye put him, though?" asked Tim.

"Around here," Tom said, pointing to a recumbent figure on the deck, with a handkerchief in his mouth and his hands and feet tied. The sailor rolled with the rise and fall of the ship and seemed most uncomfortable.

"The captain gave me a hand," Tom explained, "or else I would never have finished tying him up.

"Better keep an eye out," cautioned the mate. "Looks to me like they were going to make another try for the ladders."

"All right," the boys replied, and exchanging an encouraging slap on the back, they took up their positions.

"Holler, if you want to be saved agin," instructed Tim.

But Tom did not reply, for when he crouched down and peered at the shadow of the deckhouse, where the group was, there was something about their attitude, as nearly as he could make out, that indicated preparations for a concerted attack.

The repulse of the last assault had angered the mutineers, and they were now determined at all costs to overcome the little group on the after deck, and deal with them as they had planned.

Meanwhile, the captain had been steadily holding the ship on the shore tack, and he figured that by daylight they would be in sight of land.

The boys had not long to wait before the rush began. With a shout, the crew dashed along the deck, faltered for a moment as the three defenders fired at them, and then came on.

The boys and the mate seized another musket each, and fired once more, this time in their opponents' very faces. But those behind pushed their frightened and wounded comrades aside and started up the ladders. The larger party made for Tom, while just enough to make things interesting surged up and down the ladder that Tim and the mate were guarding. Had one of them left to aid Tom, the other would probably have been overpowered. So Tom had his hands full, and although he kept the leaders from gaining the deck, he was slowly tiring from his exertions, and he knew that before long the mutineers would have him overpowered.

Tom was growing dizzy, and the ceaseless swinging and thrusting with his musket was weakening, when from the forward hatch burst a fresh group of men shouting wildly and rushing for the rear of the mutineers. The attacking party turned to meet what they thought was a new foe, and Tom sank back against the cabin thoroughly exhausted.

"She's afire! Save yourselves!" the new arrivals were shouting. "She's afire! The hold is burning!"

The words came dimly to Tom's ears, and he dropped to the deck with a feeling that at last rest had come, and all was over.

But not for long. Tim and the mate came upon him lying there, and picking him up bodily, carried him to the rail. There the captain was working desperately over the boat on the davits, and the mate turned to help him. In a few moments they had the ropes loosed, and placing Tom in the bottom of the boat they all climbed in and lowered away. The dory struck the water, rose on the next wave, and was away from the ship. They pulled out the oars from under the seats, put them in place and rowed away. The sailors were rushing wildly about the decks seeking some means of escape.

"Great heavens!" ejaculated the captain. "That hold's full of powder. They'll all be blown to kingdom come!"

The little party were staggered by this sudden destruction that was overtaking their enemies, but there was nothing they could do, and they must save themselves. The rowers redoubled their efforts, and before they had gotten any great distance from the doomed vessel the waters were shaken with a great blast, and a pillar of flame shot up into the night, and the light showed the two halves of the ship split apart, with the balance of the sailors clinging to the wreckage and trying to climb aboard the floating skeleton of the wreck.

CHAPTER VI
ON THE MARCH.

The long fight and their narrow escape had so tired Dick and Fritz that after going a few miles further, the two Patriots decided to make camp and get a much needed rest. They had gotten fairly well along on their trip, and in spite of their forced halts had covered a good deal of ground.

The boys turned aside from the road; dismounted and leading their horses, struck into the woods for a space. When they had reached a slight hollow far enough from the path of travel, to conceal their fire, they threw off their kits, and undertook the preparation of a meal.

Dick cut a few strips of bacon, kneaded a cup full of flour, and set Fritz to gathering dry leaves, twigs and heavy wood to keep the fire blazing. They were both dog-tired, but neither uttered the slightest complaint, and by the time the coffee was bubbling and the bacon sizzling over the camp fire both boys felt a great deal better, and fell to with keen appetites on their rough meal.

"This is better than taking any chances at a farm house," said Dick. "Those soldiers we chased to-day may come back along this road, and we might get into their clutches again. I don't think we would get out as easily next time."

"Vat mit climbin' chimneys, und hidin' unter straw heabs, und running und fightin'—"

"Anything else you can think of, Fritz?" asked Dick, laughingly, as Fritz stopped for breath.

"Vat happened is happened, anyhow," said Fritz, "und it's a good thing dot Irisher Tim vasn't along to get us into more troubles."

Dick roared at this comment on their friend, and refused to spoil the joke by telling the German what he was laughing at. It was plain that Fritz accounted himself a skilful messenger, and didn't see that part of their troubles had been occasioned by his own good intentioned, but ill-considered acts.

The boys talked for a while, and then when the night grew chilly they rolled up singly in their blankets and soon dropped off to sleep.

For a wonder they passed the night in peace and quiet. Either the English had passed them in the dark, or they hadn't gotten up enough enterprise to prompt them to renew the pursuit after their defeat that afternoon.

The rising sun saw the boys up and ready for their march. A dip into the nearby creek, a hasty breakfast, and they were off on their trip to Vincennes.

At noon that day they rode boldly up to the door of a farm house, and asked a surly looking grey-haired farmer for a meal, for which they would gladly pay what was fair. The man's face brightened visibly at the mention of payment, and after looking them over again, he drawled, "Wall, I reckon you two young uns kin get a bit here, providin' you're able to pay fer it."

"Sure," answered Fritz, holding out a handful of coin with which he was equipped for traveling.

The man's eyes narrowed a little at the sight of the money, but he didn't express any surprise, and nodding toward the stable, said, "Just stow your nags in there and come in. We'll have somethin' ready in a minit."

As they turned toward the stable Dick thought he saw another form through the half-open door of the kitchen, but the vision was so uncertain that he dismissed the thought and busied himself with his horse.

"Dot money opened the old crab's eyes, yes?" chuckled Fritz.

"Seemed to me he closed them," said Dick. "I'm afraid it isn't wise to show more than one coin at a time, Fritz."

"Dot old feller couldn't do notings," boasted the German boy. "And besides I don't always got so much to show."

"Oh, I guess everything is all right," replied Dick, "but I thought the old man looked rather interested at your display of good money."

"Veil, id don't do him any no good," returned Fritz. "He gets enough for vat fer meals he gives us, und dot's all."

The boys now walked up to the house, and entered the kitchen. Again Dick thought he saw someone in the front room, but he couldn't investigate, and besides, what of it? There were undoubtedly others in the house.

The farmer appeared to have prepared the meal himself, and as he set it before them he plied them with questions.

"Bin fightin'?" he queried.

"Some," replied Dick, his mouth full of hot potato.

"Which side?" asked the farmer.

"Patriot, of course."

"Of course," agreed the old man.

"Sure," said Fritz, and Dick kicked him in the shins.

"Hear them British is about knocked out," continued their host.

"They will be before long," Dick answered. "They are getting enough of this chasing up and down the country, and finding food scarce and enemies plentiful."

"They ain't all enemies, though."

"No, there are a few good for nothing Tories left," said Dick.

"That's kind o' hard talk," the old man drawled.

"They ought to be called worse than that," Dick returned sharply.

"S'pose I was one, myself?"

Fritz choked at the very thought of such a possibility, and Dick began to look about for the cause of the farmer's long conversation. At that instant there came a long whistle from outside the house, and with a bound the farmer reached the door and stood in front of it. Dick sprang from his stool, grabbed the old man roughly about the shoulders, and hurled him from his position at the door. He ran outside, followed by Fritz, who had started to his comrade's assistance, and discovered their two horses going at a gallop down the road, led by a young man on a third horse.

"So that's their little game," cried Dick.

"Come on, ve'll catch him," yelled Fritz, and started headlong in pursuit.

Dick ran with him, but it was soon evident to both of them that the longer they ran the farther behind they got. So they slowed down to a walk, and as they reached the top of a long wooded hill, they stopped to get their breath.

"I'll climb up that old tree, I guess," said Dick. "Maybe we can see something of the rascals from the top."

"Yah, und I'll go too up," commented Fritz.

So the two started climbing, and Dick gradually worked his way toward the upper branches of an aged oak. When he had almost reached the top he heard a loud crash, and looking below saw his good friend land with a dull thud on the mossy ground beneath.

"What's the trouble?" called Dick.

"Troubles enough," responded the startled boy. "Dot old tree is so shaky dot I don't see how you up climbed him."

This statement occasioned so much laughter on Dick's part, that the old monarch of the forest in retribution pretty nearly landed him on the ground beside Fritz, and it was only by hurriedly grasping the nearest branches and steadying himself that Dick retained his position.

"Veil, vhere is he at?" questioned Fritz, referring to the person whom they had seen making away with their horses.

"Can't see him at all," Dick replied, scanning the road for a view of the vanished horseman. "That's funny, too, Fritz, for I can see way ahead of where he should be."

"Maype he is hiding," conjectured the German.

"By George!" ejaculated Dick.

"How do you know his name?" asked Fritz.

"Don't," responded Dick. "Look here, Fritz. There is another road running parallel with this one, a little further down in the valley."

"Vell, dot don't help us any yet," replied Fritz. "One road is enough to valk on. No, yes?"

"But I'll bet it does help us, you lazy goose. That fellow may have gone across to it through the woods, and if we hurry, we'll head him off."

Dick came down rapidly and the two rushed off through the brush and timber toward the road which Dick had discovered.

"Be a little careful about making any noise," cautioned Dick. "If that fellow hears us floundering about in this way, he will take alarm and ride off again, and then where would all your tree climbing and running help you?"

"Py golly, running is bad, but no more shaky trees for me," replied Fritz.

They could now see the opening ahead of them where the road ran through. It was a rough log track, and unless in a desperate hurry, no one would think of galloping over it. The two boys crouched behind the wall of foliage that reached to the road's edge, and were almost ready to abandon all hope of meeting their man, when from down the road came the sound of whistling, and presently the young Tory and the trio of horses came in sight.

The youth evidently assumed that he was now perfectly safe from pursuit, and was proceeding leisurely back to the farm house with his prize. Probably he would have soon left the horses in the woods, and then have gone to the farm house alone to get the lay of the land, but if such had been his intention, it was rudely interrupted by the two Patriots whose mounts he was so calmly leading.

With a shout which could be heard a mile, Dick and Fritz leaped from their ambush and grasped the startled Tory's horse. Fritz held tight to the bit and Dick grabbed the young farmer by the leg and pulled him out of the saddle.

Dick then proceeded to administer a sound and much deserved thrashing to the cause of their trouble, and when the young fellow recovered partially from his surprise, he broke away and started on a dead run for the farm house. Dick had neither time or desire to pursue him, and was well satisfied with recovering their steeds, and Fritz was particularly delighted with the addition of one horse to their party. The Tory was well out of reach by now, and before he turned to dive into the safety of the woods, he shouted, placing his hands to his mouth to form a megaphone, "Next time I'll get you, you rebels!"

"That fellow seems familiar to me somehow," said Dick. "I wonder where we've seen him before?"

"Oh—ah—I've got it," stuttered Fritz.

"Got what?" asked Dick.

"Dot's the same feller you pushed in the ditch already, the day we started out."

"You're right," answered Dick. "That's who it is."

"Sure, I'm right," returned Fritz, as if such was always the case.

"I wonder what he's doing here. He must have followed us after that little meeting we first had. Do you know, Fritz, I believe that fellow has been responsible for the close attention we have been getting all along the line. But what can his object be?"

This was too much for Fritz's detective powers, and he gave up the matter as beyond explanation. But Dick didn't, and it bothered him for some time as they rode rapidly along with their captive horse tugging at the line behind them.

The log road seemed to take the right direction, and rather than search through the woods for the main highway, the boys held to it. It was comfortable riding here too, and the overhanging branches served to keep the hot afternoon sun from bothering the travelers.

The boys rode in silence, broken only by occasional comments upon their stormy trip thus far, and sometimes they spoke of the small wild furry folk scampering away through the underbrush aroused by the intrusion of these strangers upon their domains.

The calm of a warm summer afternoon in the forest settled upon the boys, and they were both glad of the relief, after their continued excitement and vigilance. Dick's thoughts traveled back to their home up north, and lingered longer than necessary on a very close relative of Ben Foster's, namely, Ben's sister. And when he recovered with a guilty start from those pleasant memories, his mind roamed again to Ben, himself, lying in the Charleston hospital, with Tom and Tim, bless them, watching over him.

They, too, were perhaps under way by this time and before long they would either meet where the trail struck in across the mountains, or they would be traveling very closely after one another. And yet, in the unforeseen future, one of them might fail to complete that journey. But no, Dick refused to entertain such discouraging thoughts.

Dick came to with a start. He had been dozing there in the shade of the great forest trees; in fact, Fritz was still half asleep in his saddle. The horses had walked steadily on, all this time, however, and now they were back in the main roadway again.

"Wake up, old man!" called Dick.

"Yah. Um," yawned Fritz, coming back to earth.

"We have got to keep our eyes open, now," said Dick.

And they did, until some time after night fall, when both of them, tired with the day's march, climbed from their saddles, walked back into the sparsely covered timber land with their horses, and prepared for another night in the open.

CHAPTER VII
ON THE BEACH.

The day was just beginning to break in the East when the little wave-tossed boat bearing the Patriot survivors of the ill-fated ship, drew in sight of land. The first bright rays of the rising sun showed the low fringe of shore to the four in the boat, and it was a very welcome sight indeed. Tom had now recovered his strength, and was anxious to take his place at the oars, but although his comrades were tired out with several hours' rowing, they refused to allow him to exert himself till he had fully recovered from the strain of the night's battle. Tom's part in that fight had been the hardest, and he had certainly shown himself to be a true Dare, fearless and strong in all circumstances.

As the light grew stronger, Tim, who was in the bow, exclaimed, "Faith, and it seems to me they are cooking our breakfast for us."

Although the rest had no idea who "they" referred to, all looked towards the distant shore, and it seemed, as Tim had said, that several thin streams of smoke were rising and joining into a heavier column above the treetops.

"Looks like signs of an encampment," said Tom. "I wonder whether they are friends or enemies?"

"Frinds or inimies makes no difference at all," answered Tim. "We'll not be able to keep on cruising in this little tub much longer, and if they are inimies sure we'll be after tellin' them we have but just left a good boat belongin' to the sailors of King George, which will be but the plain truth, and that of all the grand company that sailed to fight the inimies of the King, we are the only ones left."

"It might be a wise thing to evade arrest or imprisonment if they are English troops," said Tom, "but we'll hope they are Patriots till we know to the contrary. What do you think about it, captain?"

"Well, it's certain that I don't want to be penned up till the end of this war, and it seems to me that if we all stick to Tim's story, we may remove any suspicion and be allowed our liberty."

"Sure, and in this game it's only right and proper to keep your liberty," replied Tim. "And remember, Tom, you have got work ahead of you before we get to——"

"Where we are going," interposed Tom, quickly, anxious to have everything regarding his journey kept as secret as possible. He knew that the mate and the captain were perfectly loyal to the cause, but his instructions were to keep his destination to himself, and he intended to do so.

Tim, thus admonished, said no more.

The boat had drawn nearer the shore now, and all four were keenly and somewhat anxiously watching the beach for signs of the men they knew must be there.

They had not long to wait, for in a few minutes a whole company tumbled out of the woods and ran down to the beach for their morning swim. As they were in the act of undressing, one of them caught sight of a boat containing the Patriots.

"Hi, there, comrades," he shouted, "we are having early visitors."

Several of the men ran back for their rifles, and so Tom stuck up an oar with his handkerchief knotted at the end of it, as a signal of friendship. The mate and Tim pulled straight for the group on the beach.

"Better make it seem as though we are glad to see them," the mate suggested. "If they take us for Tories, we will be free to go our own way, but if they suspect our real feelings we will certainly be in trouble."

So they rowed steadily shoreward, pointing the nose of their little craft for the group of British troops.

"Ahoy on shore!" shouted Tim. "We are after comin' from his majesty's royal fleet, and want to spake with your officers."

Tim grinned as he shouted this, and all the party wondered how his story would be taken.

"You'll see them quick enough," replied one of the Redcoats. "Plenty quick enough if you are friends of his majesty's—God bless him—and too quick if you are not."

Some of the soldiers ran out into the surf and pulled the boat in when they had about reached the beach, and with many expressions of thankfulness and apparent joy the Patriots tumbled out and joined the English.

"We are the last of a strong little crew and a good ship," volunteered the captain. "The other poor boys went down with the ship."

"And what may you be doing here, when, as far as I can see, a captain is supposed to stick till the last?"

"We were rowing about, trying to pick up this man who had fallen overboard," invented the captain, who had been caught in a peculiar position. In fact, as this instance shows, and as the boys well knew, it is both unwise and difficult to attempt deception, even in a good cause.

"A likely thing to my way of thinking," said the soldier. "Captains do not generally go overboard after sailors when they fall over, do they?"

"Not generally," said Tom. "But the captain and I had been good friends, and he was anxious to save me quickly."

"Guess this must be a matter for the officers," said one of the men. "They will pretty soon find out whether these fellows are what they claim to be or not."

Now, Tom had a great dislike for being seen by the officers, for his activities with Dick had often thrown him into the enemy's hands, and he was afraid that some of his former captors might be with this party. Therefore to gain a little time, he said, "Now, see here, boys, everything you will find to be all right and satisfactory, and before we go to see the general or whoever it is that has command, we would like to take a dip in the surf and get freshened up a bit. Rowing around all night in an open boat doesn't help your appearance any, and we'll just join you boys in a swim, if you don't mind. Then we'll all be ready to go up and straighten things out."

"That's all right, young feller," said the spokesman of the troops, a corporal, "you can have your swim all right, but don't you be too sure it will be as easy to straighten things out as you think."

"Good," said Tom. "That's fine. And we'll be able to explain everything later on."

Meanwhile, Tom's mind had been working rapidly, and he saw that they would easily ferret out the truth of the story as long as there were four of them to question. He didn't see how Tim and he could be any worse off by facing the matter out. It was about time for Dick and Fritz to be along in that part of the country, too, for their trip overland would take them longer than Tom had taken, being driven rapidly up the coast by the storm. Therefore, it seemed to him that if he could manage to get the captain and the mate out of the way, it would be better all around. So, when the party prepared to remove their clothes, Tom whispered to the captain:

"Captain, we can't stop to argue matters out to form any detailed plan, but Tim and I will start some kind of a fuss in the water now, and while we keep their attention, you and the mate float quietly down the shore on your backs till you reach those plum bushes—see them?—those beach plums down there." Tom motioned with his eyes. "It's a great joke being taken for rebels isn't it?" he said in a louder voice as a soldier approached. "One would think we looked like desperadoes."

The captain smiled and nodded his head, and Tom saw that he was answering his instructions.

"Come along, you fellows," shouted the corporal, "we haven't got all morning for this swim."

"All right. We're ready," answered Tom, and they all trotted down to the water's edge.

"Gee, it's cold," chattered Tom.

"Faith, and if your lordship will wait a moment, I'll warm it for you," replied Tim, giving Tom a vigorous push that sent him floundering out to his waist.

"I'll fix you for that," shouted Tom, seeing that Tim had unconsciously started the excitement that he wanted.

Tom ran back and headed Tim up the shore away from the plum bushes. They raced about fifty yards, and at the shout of the soldiers, who were all watching their antics with interest, Tim ducked and rushed out into the water. Tom was on his heels and they began a spirited water-fight, of which Tim soon had enough, and he turned and dove through an oncoming wave and struck out lustily to evade Tom.

Things were working out better than Tom had expected, and the soldiers, amused by the spirited fight the two boys were waging, followed them up the beach and gave the mate and the captain an excellent chance to scurry down the water line with their clothes in their hands.

Tom, keeping far enough from Tim to encourage him, and yet near enough to keep the interest of the troopers, saw the naked figures go out of sight around a sand dune near the beach plums. If he could only give them a few more minutes they would be safe, and after some more running, and a moment's stop to don their clothes, would be out of the soldier's reach. And Tom didn't imagine that they would ever let the troops get close enough to catch them, either.

"I've got you now, you Irish villain," he yelled at the sputtering Tim. Tom reached out and caught the flying foot in front of him, and in a minute had Tim ducked head-foremost under the water.

The soldiers set up a shout of laughter at this, and letting Tim come to the surface, Tom renewed the splash-fight, treading meanwhile with his feet. Tim, however had had quite enough by this time, and was heading for land as fast as his tired arms and legs would propel him.

He arrived sputtering and breathless, and shouted as best he could with a mouth full of salt water, "Enough. I've got enough, you old duck. Just 'cause I give you a friendly pat, up you go and chase me over the face of the whole earth."

"If that was a friendly pat, I'm glad you didn't push me hard," replied Tom, laughing.

A bugle rang out in the woods just then, and the men made a hasty dive for their clothes, some of them not even stopping to dry perfectly. While they were rushing around, a group of officers appeared at the edge of the timber on their way to the beach.

"Where are those other two?" suddenly queried the corporal, recalled to his sense of duty by the appearance of the officers.

"Gone on up to the camp, I suppose," said Tim. "Sure, an' if they were as hungry as me they would be eating ye out of house and home by now."

Tom felt that by this time the two sailors had gotten a fair start, and his spirits were rising proportionately, when of a sudden a shot, followed by several scattering reports, rang out.

"Come along, you two!" shouted the corporal, and the two boys were hustled unceremoniously up the beach, donning their clothes as best they could while trotting along. The officers had turned and dashed back toward the encampment, and when the soldiers with their captives reached there the whole place was in confusion, with troops rushing in all directions, shouting and firing their muskets at random into the woods.

"This cooks our goose," said Tom. "They are evidently disturbed at something, and I can see where we come in for our share of the trouble."

"It must be the captain and the mate they are blazing at," suggested Tim. "Sure, and they will never hit a thing at all at the rate they are firin' and rushin' around."

"I hope they don't," said Tom.

"Come this way, ye rebels!" bellowed the excited corporal.

"Don't pay any attention when he calls us rebels," said Tom. "Don't let him see that we recognize the name at all."

At their apparent indifference to his commands, the corporal ran up and grasping them each by an arm, hurried up to the central tent. An officer in a major's uniform was talking to a young man as they were brought up, and gave no heed to their presence till he was finished.

The boys listened eagerly, and were greatly astonished to hear what was going on between the two.

"A piece of rank carelessness on the part of the men," the major was saying. "They were both securely guarded, and should never have escaped, but the minute our backs are turned these hired troops forget their duty, and everything else but themselves, and give those rascals a chance that they didn't overlook."

"There'll be the dickens to pay when this gets to headquarters," said the young fellow in civilian's clothes. "We have got to get them again, or we will have to pay for it. I've followed those two for a full week or more, and had them almost secure three times, and every time they slip away when they seem safest. When we get them again we'll have to let nothing stand in the way of their safe return to Charleston."

"Don't worry, we'll get them again," returned the major. "With this force at our disposal, two young fellows like that can never successfully escape us for long."

"They better not or we might as well stay away too," replied the young man. "And, besides, I have a little personal matter to settle with one of them."

"So that's what makes you so anxious to get them, is it?" queried the officer.

"That makes me doubly anxious," answered the younger man.

"Do you know who they are talking about?" asked Tom, in a whisper.

"Sure, and it must be Dick Dare and Fritz," answered Tim.

CHAPTER VIII
THE AMBUSH.

Dick Dare and Fritz journeyed for several days without anything happening to impede their progress, and they had made up most of the time that had been lost in their earlier escapades. They took no chances at night and slept out in the open rather than risk capture or trouble in a farm house.

Their midday meals they had bought from farmers, and had eaten them standing by their horses, not caring to experience another loss of those faithful animals.

The boys' spirits rose with their long freedom from trouble, and although they still kept a sharp outlook for signs of the enemy, they didn't find anything to disturb them.

If it had not been for Dick's persistent efforts to hurry, Fritz would have considered the whole affair as an outing for pleasure only, but as it was, their hard traveling and short rests kept him always on the go, and he never felt that he had had quite enough sleep. Dick was tireless and seemed only to think of the haste they were in, and pushed ahead for Vincennes relentlessly. Their long immunity from trouble had lulled Dick into too great a sense of safety, and it was while eating their supper one evening by the roadside that the boys were startled by a bugle call in the woods which lay back of them.

They jumped to their feet, seized the bridles, and climbing hastily into their saddles, started full tilt up the road. Almost instantly a party Redcoats stepped out and halted their progress in that direction. Wheeling hastily, the boys covered about a hundred yards back, fearing that at any moment a volley would follow them, but not a gun was fired, and just as they began to feel new hope, another group of soldiers appeared before them, blocking their way completely.

Dick turned desperately toward the fences at the roadside, but the road was lined with Redcoated, grinning troopers.

"An ambush!" cried Dick.

"Trapped good and proper this time, young feller," observed a corporal, smiling with satisfaction. "Guess you two have kept away from us long enough. Come along and see the major."

The boys were surrounded, and both Fritz and Dick saw that escape was out of the question at present, so both decided to take things coolly and make the best of a bad situation.

The major, accompanied by his brother officers, stood in the road as the captives were led up, and showed his satisfaction at their capture. Dick and Fritz were both startled to see the young southerner with the group, and he in particular seemed immensely pleased to get the boys again.

"You two have led us a pretty chase, and should be working in a better cause," said the major.

"But they are on the wrong side of the fence this time," said the young fellow Dick had rolled into the ditch the first day out. "And that Dare boy has been almost hanged so many times that the general will take great pleasure in finishing the job this time, I'm sure."

"It seems that we are your prisoners," said Dick, turning to the officer. "I trust you will save us the indignity of being insulted by that young boor at your side."

"Seems to be some little feeling, eh?" chuckled the officer. "All right, my young bantam, you and your friend can join the men, I guess, and we will see that your company is selected most carefully."

"Dot's imbossible, in this troop," said Fritz to Dick, but no one else heard him.

The two Patriots were placed on horseback, and with their wrists tied together, and a rope passed to two troopers the company passed on up the road.

They turned out from the main road soon and pitched camp on a wooded slope leading down to the sea, where the sound of the breakers soon lulled the tired Redcoats to sleep.

The boys were placed near a large fire, and were securely guarded. Dick and Fritz were both tired out, and after seeing that there was no immediate hope of escape or help, both rolled over and joined their captors in slumberland.

Early the next morning the camp was astir, and the boys saw the men prepare for a dip into the surf.

"It would be dandy to have a little plunge in those breakers," said Dick. "How about you, Fritz?"

"Yah, I suppose it would, but I bet it's cold," replied the German, rubbing his eyes.

"Can we go along with you men?" asked Dick.

"I'll see about it," answered one, walking toward the officers' tents.

He returned in a moment with a favorable reply, and in a jiffy the boys were racing down the sands with the first group of men.

After an invigorating plunge in the cold waves, the boys dressed and returned to the camp. All there were astir by now, and the two prisoners were conducted to the centre of the encampment and left in charge of two soldiers. Various groups were assembled about their respective fires, and all were eagerly hastening the preparation of their morning meal. From each group certain ones were despatched into the surrounding forest to gather a liberal supply of firewood, while others measured out portions of coffee, flour and bacon.

The cooks fussed importantly over the fires, ordering the men about in tones they would not dare to use when away from their important positions. At meal times the cooks of a camp are always the autocrats.

Dick and Fritz sniffed the air hungrily and thanked fortune that at least they would not be starved to death.

"There doesn't seem to be any hope of escape just now, does there?" said Dick.

Fritz wrinkled up his nose and gazed thoughtfully about him.

"For myself, I don't care about escapes till after we eat somedings," he returned.

"Then you had better eat it soon," Dick commented, "for if we get a chance we won't stay around for breakfast. The rest of the troop are all going down to the water now, and if we have any opportunity at all this morning it is apt to come now."

As Dick had said, the balance of the troop, by far the largest part, were leaving for a dip in the ocean, while the breakfast preparations and prisoners were left in charge of the first little company who had gone in when the boys did.

"Let's wander over by the beach and watch the crowd," suggested Dick.

"All right. Dot's as good as anyding, only I would like to hurry those cooks again yet," replied Fritz. "Dot cooking of bacons is bad for my appetite, already. If they don't make it done soon already I would eat it unraw."

"You're mighty particular about your food, seeing you're a prisoner," laughed Dick.

"In this war it is no fair to torture prisoners," answered Fritz with spirit. "Und dat's what those Redgoats is doing me to."

"Look at that out there!" exclaimed Dick Dare, pointing as he spoke to a little dark spot bobbing on the waves in the distance. The boys had reached the edge of the trees by now, and were forbidden by the soldiers to go any further.

Fritz shaded his eyes with both hands and squinted in the direction indicated by Dick.

"Looks like a log," said Fritz.

"Not to me," replied Dick. "Seems to me that there are people in a small boat. Wonder what they can possibly be doing out there at this time of the morning?"

"Dot's right. It's peobles!" exclaimed Fritz. "Und they are goming this way."

The boys watched the approach of the boat with great interest, and when the party on board stood up to disembark, Dick Dare gave a sudden start.

"That's funny, but it can't be them," he muttered.

"Fritz, do you see anything familiar about the figures in the boat?" he questioned in an eager whisper.

Before Fritz could study the landing party more closely, the two boys were ordered back to the camp fires, and try as they might to get another view of the beach, and the new arrivals, they were unable to move far enough away from their guards to do so.

"That's bad luck," grumbled Dick. "I had an idea that Tim and Tom were in that boat. But just when we might have been able to make them out, off we are hustled, and I don't know now whether it was them or not."

"If it was, they will be here plenty soon enough," said Fritz. "And then when we are all together once, who will get to Vincennes in dime already?"

"That would be bad," said Dick, seriously. "If this one group of soldiers should round up both parties of us, I'm afraid the general's message will never get through, and we'll all swing for our past adventures in this awful war. But come, don't let's worry about things that we are only guessing at. That may not be Tom and Tim, and really, I don't see how it could be."

For about fifteen minutes nothing new happened, and Fritz and Dick began to hope that Dick had been mistaken in his surmise that Tom and Tim were coming ashore.

Then of a sudden they heard a great crashing in the woods where the horses were tethered, and shouts of, "I'm aboard, mate," and "Shake 'em out, captain," came plainly to their ears through the trees.

The soldiers about the fires grabbed up their guns and dashed into the woods toward the horses, and the boys could see for one brief instant two galloping forms go thundering off through the woods toward the road. The muskets cracked and the troopers shouted dire threats at the two men, but although the chase soon drew out of sight, Dick didn't think that either of the men had been hit, and at the rate they were going he was quite sure that they would not be overtaken.

The excitement of the moment had left Dick without thought for his own situation, and it was Fritz who realized that for a moment they were alone. He heard the officers returning to camp from the beach, and grabbing Dick by the arm, he scurried off in a direction half way between that taken by the pursuing soldiers and returning officers.

"Nefer mind the breakfast," Fritz cried, abandoning his greatest need in the excitement. "Let us out get."

"Good boy," exclaimed Dick. "You have your wits with you to-day, for sure."

They had no time to talk further, however. The returning soldiers would soon be hard on their trail, and without horses, they had but a slim chance of making good their escape. The confusion, and the two parties, however, helped them more than they had hoped. They reached the road, crossed it and entered the woods on the other side without being seen.

Dick and Fritz ran on until they felt that if they did not rest soon their heads would burst. Stumbling along, keeping the sun over their right shoulders they finally came out upon a great body of water. It was the Chesapeake, and both of them dropped flat on their stomachs and bathed their tired heads in the cold salt water.

"This is all right, if we can only get a canoe now," said Dick, standing up and feeling greatly refreshed.

"It don't look so very fine to me," replied Fritz. "We are here together, yet with nothing to eat, nothing to shoot with und nothing to go somewheres with——"

"Nothing to be hung with either. You better remember that and be happy," said Dick. "We were comfortable in the British camp, maybe, but we had a noose waiting for us sooner or later, you know."

"Und ve'll keep it vaiting already," responded Fritz, very much cheered by this viewpoint.

CHAPTER IX
IN CAMP.

"Bring those two in here," said the major to the corporal, who was holding Tom Dare and Tim.

He retired to the tent, and sat down on a small stool beside a camp table. The boys were pushed forward into the tent and stood before the British officer. There was no fear in their glances, and in fact they seemed the coolest members of the party.

"What have got to say for yourselves?" questioned the major severely.

"What have we got to say for ourselves?" repeated Tom, speaking to gain time.

"That's what I said!" snapped the officer. "Come now! Who are you? What are you doing here, and what explanation can you make for the escape of your two companions?"

"Praises be!" shouted Tim. "So they did escape?"

"Only temporarily," replied the major. "And kindly remember, young man, that you are in the presence of an officer of his British Majesty, and we don't permit interruptions from prisoners."

"That last expression explains our standing in this company, I presume," said Tom. "May I ask why we are considered as prisoners, when there seems to be no apparent ground for holding us?"

"There is plenty of reason for holding you two prisoners," replied the officer. "You came ashore without any good reason for being out in an open boat all night. Your two companions escaped for the time being after stealing two of our horses, and in the excitement two very important prisoners managed to slip away from their guards, thus causing us any amount of unnecessary trouble and annoyance. You have a good deal to answer for and no good answers to give as far as I can see."

"Well, to begin with, we were the survivors of a wreck. Our ship blew up, and the captain, mate, my friend and I escaped in the dory that we landed in," replied Tom. "I guess our reception was not cordial enough to inspire the other two with any desire to stay, and they just departed by the easiest route they could find. I don't see why we should be held responsible for their actions, nor for the escape of your other prisoners."

"Where were you bound when you were wrecked?" questioned their captor.

"New York," replied Tom, doing some hasty thinking. "We were going to land and go down to Philadelphia, where we live, after transacting some business in New York."

"What took you so far from home?" queried the major.

"We worked our way down on a coasting schooner," replied Tom, referring to a previous experience, and trying desperately to lighten the aspect of the bad situation they had fallen into.

"Your story isn't convincing enough," replied the officer, and Tom's heart sank at his words. "I think we'll keep you with us for awhile, and see what else we can find out about you. You look a whole lot like that very slippery rebel spy we are chasing, and maybe you know him."

"Who is that?" asked Tom, with apparent indifference.

"Dick Dare," replied the major, watching Tom closely.

But Tom was already sure of whom was meant and never blinked an eyelash.

"You boys can join the troops," continued the major, "and understand that any attempt to escape will be at your own risk. I think you will bear a little watching."

"I want to protest against such treatment," Tom said hotly, "and if we get the opportunity, I will report this to those who will make you regret this affair."

With that he and Tim walked out of the tent and sauntered over to a fire. The soldiers were finishing their interrupted breakfast, and at a nod from their old acquaintance, the corporal, the boys sat down and joined them. Both of them were famished and the food was very welcome.

Shortly after the meal was over, camp was struck, and the boys were given horses to ride and instructed to keep in the centre of the troop.

"These look like Dick's and Fritz's horses," said Tom. "They haven't any of the usual army trappings, and the equipment seems different from the rest."

Two of the troopers rode in the camp wagon, as their horses had been appropriated by the mate and the captain in their dash for freedom. Tom and Tim were considered more secure on horseback and in the centre of the troop.

The party rode to the edge of the bay along the road, and then several of them dismounted and closely inspected the shore for traces of any of their fugitive's footsteps. They had only gone about half a mile in this fashion when they came upon footprints leading to the water's edge. It was here that Dick and Fritz had rested after their long run through the woods. The spot where they had come out and marks down to the water's edge were all that the troopers could find, and as there was no sign of a boat having landed or pushed off, the officers decided that the boys had kept in the shallow water near shore to hide their further trail.

The troop, was therefore, ordered forward, and all the forenoon they cantered briskly along the shore road, following the turns and twistings of the irregular shore line, and making frequent detours to avoid the deeper creeks that ran into the bay. They did not stop but for a few moments at noon, when a hasty bite was snatched by the men and horses, and the latter were given a breathing spell.

Still there was no sign of the fugitives, and the two boys, Tom and Tim, were as elated as their companions were discouraged.

"Dick and Fritz must have gone the other way," said Tim, late in the afternoon.

"Or else they got hold of a boat of some kind," said Tom. "I am inclined to think it was the latter, for the other direction would have led them back toward the camp, and would have delayed them further on their journey. If these good fellows only keep going at this rate they will get us within striking distance of our destination."

"And thim never guessing how kind they are," chuckled Tim. "If they only knew how glad we are to go along they would probably face about and cart us back agin."

"We must try to gain their confidence," Tom went on, quietly. "If they do get hot on Dick's trail, and we are free to give them warning, we can be of more use staying with them than by escaping."

"Thot's a foine idea," said Tim, greatly pleased with the new turn things had taken.

"And, of course, at the end of the chase, if it only lasts that long, we'll try to make our escape, and get to Vincennes with Dick and Fritz. But I suppose that's almost too much to expect."

"Oi don't know, now. This pack of hounds seems moighty anxious to catch up with your brother and the Dootchman, and Oi'm after thinkin' they'll stay roight along to the ind of the chase."

"Let's hope the chase only ends in Vincennes then," replied Tom, hopefully.

That night the British party were able to make out the lights of several camp fires across the bay. The day's trip had brought them near the head waters of the Chesapeake, and across the narrower portion of the water the glitter of the fires could be easily distinguished. A council was held by the officers and they determined to make an early start in the morning and endeavor to reach the end of the bay before the party on the opposite shore, so that if their prey were with the other group and traveling in the same direction, they might be within striking distance.

The night passed without adventure and the two boys made considerable progress toward getting friendly with the troopers by relating stories while seated about the fires in the evening. From the talk of the soldiers, carefully guided by veiled hints from Tom, they learned the history of Dick Dare's and Fritz's adventures since they had left Charleston.

The soldiers recounted their many encounters with the two energetic Patriots and were especially bitter about their defeat by the boys and their friends some days back on the road. Tom and his companion could scarcely refrain from laughing at the thought that these men were so innocently telling Dick's own brother and one of his closest friends how these two trouble makers had outwitted the forces of his royal majesty, King George the Third.

The troopers soon tired of telling of their poor success with Dick and Fritz, however, and rather than seem too curious about the other boys, Tim encouraged one of them to tell a story of one of the European wars that the troop had engaged in.

The man was noted for his odd tales and needed but sufficient coaxing and an appreciative audience to launch into one of his yarns.

"All right," the soldier replied to Tim's urging. "Some of us boys were in the regiment when this happened, and remember the incident, but if they can stand for an old story, I'll let you have it."

"Go ahead," said two of the older men. "You can make an old tale sound new, anyhow."

Thus encouraged the soldier launched forth on his yarn.

"It was a strange regiment, that old one, of 'Dragoons,'" he began. "There were men of all lands in that band and under the 'Red Colonel' it was a rare fighting force. We were always in the front of everything and when finally a ten days' truce with the French was decided, we were all glad of the rest.

"There was only one Spaniard, I forgot to say, in the whole regiment, for somehow or other, those fellows weren't much in favor of us and we didn't trust them any too fully. This fellow had been with us for a number of years and had time and again proven himself true to the regiment and his comrades.

"We were just at the foot of the pass through the Pyrannees when the truce came, and this Spaniard fellow, who was a captain then, and very friendly with the colonel, asked for a ten-day leave of absence. He gave some excuse about long absence from home and about going to see his mother, and the colonel allowed him to go. He took his sword and his musket with him and disappeared along the track toward the mountain passes.

"There were some in his own troop who didn't love their captain any to well and in particular the young lieutenant who was directly under this Spanish captain would have been glad to have him out of the way. Therefore, before half of his ten days were up, reports of an ugly nature began to circulate. They were somewhat to the effect that the captain had accepted an offer from our enemies and had gone over to them with information that would be of great advantage when the truce was over.

"His friends indignantly rejected all such suggestions and said that the captain himself would deal with the parties who started such rumors when he returned. But the ninth and then the tenth day came and passed and the captain didn't return to his place in the regiment, nor to disprove all remarks that had been passed in his absence.

"After twelve days, the colonel, very much against his wishes, but in accordance with his duty, had the captain deposed from office and read out of the regiment."

Here the soldier paused, and Tim, who was very much absorbed in the narrative, said, "And did the man niver turn up agin?"

"Oh, to be sure," continued the British trooper, "and that's the story. On the thirteenth night there comes a challenge from one of the outposts and the Spanish captain answers the call.

"'Halt!' says the guard. 'Who goes there!'

"'Friend,' replied the captain. 'I'm captain of troop B.'

"'Captain Thornton is captain of Troop B,' replied the sentry. 'You are no longer a member of this regiment. They read you out of it yesterday.'

"The colonel had been attracted by this disturbance and he ordered the former captain to be brought before him in his tent.

"'Well, what made you break your promise in this way?' queried his anxious superior.

"'I couldn't help it,' replied the captain. 'I was afraid when I asked for leave that if I gave the right reason you wouldn't let me go, so I said it was to visit my mother. But she has been dead for two years now. In our mountain country of Northern Spain we have what you call blood-feuds, and when they are once started the end only comes with the extinction of one or both families concerned. In our family there has been such a feud now for twenty years, but it is no more.'

"'Go on,' said the colonel, 'explain your over long absence.'

"'That was the cause of it,' continued the captain. 'I received word that the last two men, the only ones left of our enemies had been seen about my house and that my wife and two children were in danger. I hurried to their aid. In crossing the pass I lost my musket and succeeded only in reaching my house in the dark, without any firearm. There was but one old gun in the house, and, worse luck, there was but one charge for that. However, our enemies who were trying to starve out my family, didn't know of my arrival. I waited day after day, hoping, sometime, to get them both in line and to kill them with but a single shot. Day after day they went for water at the well, and lurked about the grounds around the house, but never did the chance I was waiting for present itself. Then finally, on the eleventh day of my furlough, the opportunity came. And now they are both gone and I am here.'

"The colonel's face beamed with pleasure, for his confidence in the captain had been justified.

"'Thornton is captain of Troop B now,' said the colonel. 'Your leave of absence was, I remember, for twenty days, not ten. Good-night, major.'"

"So," cried Tom, "he was not only forgiven for his overstay of leave, but promoted in rank?"

"Thot's a strange story for sure," muttered Tim. "And you say it's true?"

"Absolutely," replied the British soldier, and his two old comrades nodded their assent. In the meantime the men were preparing for their night's rest. In a very few minutes the whole troop was asleep.

CHAPTER X
TELCA.

Dick and Fritz, not wishing to lose any valuable time, struck out along the shore of the bay, keeping in the shallow places and thus concealing their tracks. They searched vainly for a boat or any craft that would move them out of the path of the pursuing English troopers, but for half a mile they discovered nothing at all.

"The activity of the troops in this section must have forced everybody who owns a boat to hide it very securely," said Dick.

"Yah, and if we should get away from those fellars, and to the other shores we would have to do it svimming, I guess," replied Fritz.

"We'll get swimming enough without going out into the bay for it," said Dick. "Here we are at a creek and no way to get past but to swim for it right now."

"I hear someding," whispered Fritz suddenly, and the two boys dodged back into the marsh grasses at the mouth of the creek.

After hurriedly making themselves as inconspicuous as possible, they peered out through the grass to see what it was had alarmed them. The boys were by no means frightened, but neither of them wanted to fall into the hands of a larger party of the enemy after their recent escape.

"It's something going up the creek," said Dick. "Sounds to me like paddling!"

"Maype here is where we get our canoe yet," Fritz said, hopefully.

"Indians," whispered Dick, as a canoe rounded a bend above them. "Not on the war path either, for the squaws are with them."

"INDIANS", WHISPERED DICK.

"Can we speak mit them?" questioned Fritz, who was decidedly anxious to get into a canoe and stop this incessant walking, riding and running that had kept them so busy for so long.

"It will probably be the only chance we'll get to get across the bay," answered Dick. "I believe we may as well risk it."

The leading canoes were now abreast of the boys, and Dick and Fritz rose to their feet and hailed them. The hail was entirely unnecessary, however, for almost as soon as they had spoken the boys were covered by a dozen rifles.

"Put your hands up, palms forward," said Dick, quickly setting the example himself.

"Friends," he called to the Indians, who, despite their lack of paint, seemed very well prepared for hostilities.

"Maybe we should schnell run for the woods already," said Fritz, rather startled by the sudden display of firearms, and sorry now that he had not stayed secure in the grass.

"Too late now, Fritz," said Dick. "These fellows look all right, even if they are supplied with more arms than a regiment."

Dick and Fritz approached the edge of the creek walking waist deep in the tall marsh grass.

"Us no like Redcoats," Dick volunteered, pointing toward Fritz. "We are Americans. No like Redcoats."

"Dot's right," chimed in Fritz, trying hard to smile into the mouths of a score of threatening rifles at once, and almost dislocating his neck in the endeavor. "And what's further they don't like us, not for something— nothing, I mean——" he ended, lamely.

One of the redmen, a short, heavily built man, with fierce, dark eyes and a sharp nose, motioned to the boys to stand still while they held a short parley among themselves in a dialect that Dick could understand but little of.

"They aren't from around here," commented Dick Dare to his companion. "That dialect of theirs is a sort of a mixture as far as I can make out and there isn't much of it I remember."

"But I don'd see why we should be kept standing here all morgen, und my arms are all reatty beginning to drop off from such long holdings up of the hands."

"Better to keep them up than to have them fill us full of lead for lowering them," replied Dick, who was trying with but slight success to make out the Indians' conversation.

"What you boys want?" asked the chief, finally, when the boys were about ready to drop their hands and take the consequences.

"Want to go with our friends, the red-men, and reach other side of big water," replied Dick. "We are your friends and would like to take canoe and paddle with the great chief and his people."

The red-man was evidently flattered by Dick's speech, and after motioning to the boys to lower their hands, which Fritz did with a groan, he turned to two of the canoe parties and indicated that the boys might seat themselves in the center of the light crafts and help paddle them.

It was a long paddle across the bay and it was fortunate that the day was a calm one, or they would never have attempted the trip. As it was, it required several hours of hard paddling to reach the distant shore, and all the party gave grunts of satisfaction on arriving safely.

The Indians were aware of the proximity of the British troops when they started out, and that was their reason for going over to the opposite shore.

The squaws of the tribe all scuttled away into the woods to start their cooking, it being the custom amongst the red-men to have the women do most of the hard work. The braves drew the light birch canoes from the water and prepared to make themselves comfortable while waiting for their meal.

"You should a few lessons take from dot tall fellar," said Fritz, stretching his arms.

"What sort of lessons?" asked Dick.

"You see the way he dreats his squawk?" continued Fritz, adding syllables to his vocabulary.

"I don't see him doing anything but ordering and bossing her around."

"It you vould like, perhabs, to be the head of dot houses you and Ben's sister is going to have———"

Here Fritz dodged a pine cone and hid safely behind a tree, while Dick searched vainly for more missiles.

"I vill be goot," yelled Fritz, enjoying Dick's confusion immensely, "and nefer speak of such things any more."

"If you'll promise," said Dick, "I will forgive you this time."

At that Fritz came out from behind his tree, and linking arms with Dick they sauntered off to one of the fires. The chief was seated beside this blaze, watching the final preparations for his meal, and he motioned the boys to join him.

"Um white boys eat with Telca," he said, and Dick was pleased to find that he knew so much English, for he knew that mutual explanations and possible plans would have to be gone over by both of them, and his own ignorance of this band's peculiar dialect prevented their carrying on any extended conversation in the red-man's tongue.

"Not wait here long," said Dick, looking at the sun. "Redcoats after white men and we must hurry."

"Where are the Redcoat soldiers?" asked the chief, helping himself to some of the fish chowder and then pushing the pot toward the boys.

"We ran away from them this morning," replied Dick. "They follow us soon, along the other shore, and there are many of them, too many for even the brave redmen to fight."

"Red-man do not want to fight too many, but if not too many———" here the chief drifted off into silence, and Dick could see that he was thinking of something that boded ill for the British troops, whoever fell into his hands. Fritz as too busy by far with the bowl of chowder and some flat cakes of baked flour to pay much attention to the conversation.

"My companion's name is Fritz," said Dick, rescuing the remains of the meal from that busy party, "and my own is Dick."

The chief nodded to indicate that he understood and would remember their names.

"We are going back to our own hunting grounds," said the Indian. "We have been away for twelve moons now, and they should be ready for us once more."

"What is the matter, game all gone?" queried Dick.

"No," replied Telca, shaking his head slowly. "If white boys stay with their red friends, Telca will tell about it tonight."

"We will certainly stay as long as possible with our new friends," said Dick, "and I hope our roads are to be together. Which way do the chief and his people travel? You must be from far away, for your tongue is new to me."

"We come across the high mountains," the chief answered, pointing to the west. "We are going home, now."

"I wish we were already yet going home too," sighed Fritz.

"I thought you were glad to go on this trip," said Dick.

"Was I glad?" asked Fritz. "Of course, but I would be glad some more to get to the end and back."

"Well, we'll get there if we keep at it," replied Dick, rising. "But if we can, I think we had better start when you are ready, chief, and put as much space between us and our enemies as possible."

"We start now," agreed Telca, giving some commands in his native dialect to the other Indians. Instantly all was hurry and bustle in the camp and after gathering up the few utensils and the food, all the tribe filed off to the shore and slid the canoes out into the water. They embarked as before and were soon strung out in a long, snake-like line, keeping fairly close to the shore and paddling silently and swiftly north and west.

They continued as long as the light lasted, and when it got too dark to see things plainly at any great distance, the chief turned his canoe toward the low shore and beached it again on the sands.

The proceedings of earlier in the day for camp making were repeated and before long several little fires were twinkling in the forest and the Indians were preparing to spend the night in this spot. Their meal consisted of some smoked meat, boiled to make it tender, and some potatoes which they roasted in the hot coals of the fire. After the Indians had eaten, they all sat around one large fire, smoking the long, root pipes, filled with fragrant tobacco. Fritz and Dick didn't smoke, but they both took a few puffs from the large peace-pipe which was passed around from man to man as a token of friendship and good-will.

"Now will our friend and brother tell the Indians of his plans?" asked the chief, addressing Dick.

"Surely," replied he. "My comrade and I wish to cross the mountains to the west with all possible speed, descend the rivers on the other side and go on to the post at Vincennes."

"It is well," said Telca, "for we too are going almost as far and will travel with the white men."

"Fine!" ejaculated Dick. "Let us pledge our friendship by shaking hands."

This formality was gravely observed and after making the round of the circle Fritz and Dick resumed their places by the fire.

"And now may we know how it happens that the red-men are so far from their own lands?"

"We left to give time for the Good Spirit to free our home of one who had gone, and yet stayed in our tribe," the chief began.

"A spirit?" asked Dick, guessing that was what Telca meant.

"Yes," replied Telca, "the spirit of my daughter, who was unable to gain entrance to our happy hunting grounds, because she died away from us, and we could not send her on as all should go. On a night thirteen moons passed, in an attack by the Redcoat soldiers, she was captured. The white men lost many braves and were greatly angry over their loss. They sought revenge and to teach a lesson to the great Indian, they outdid him in cruelty. We are not as cruel as the white man when he is angry. They bound our little daughter to the horns of a great bull-moose and drove him out into the lake. Our young men were far away and we were scattered after our defeat. But, with a few of the older men, I was following their march, waiting to rescue my girl. And after they had done this awful thing we caught up to them and could hear the great animal thrashing about near the shore of the lake and could make out the burden on its head. We shot the moose, but my daughter was dead when we reached her. Every night from then on for many nights we could hear the spirit of the moose crashing about in the forests and we could hear the screams of our lost sister bound to its head. Then came a message from the Good Spirit, and Red Wing, the son of a chief and a man of wisdom, our own prophet, delivered to us the message. We were to go away from our lands for twelve moons and when we returned our sister would be in peace in the Happy Hunting Grounds beyond, and the red-man would have his chance to revenge her death. And so we return, after twelve moons of wandering, and we are to have our revenge."

"It seems terrible that any British officer could permit such a deed," said Dick, hotly, "and although the white man's God does not wish his children to seek revenge from their enemies, I can't blame you for feeling that you are entitled to it."

A chorus of grunts went around the circle of braves, and Dick felt that some day the Redcoated soldiers would pay heavily for the deed that some of their number had done.

"I vould not like to be a Red-goat, but in whatefer they get, they more yet deserve," said Fritz.

The whole party were rather depressed at the recital of their wrongs, and in a short time they rolled up in their long blankets and dropped off to sleep.

CHAPTER XI
FOLLOWING THE TRAIL.

Tim Murphy and Tom Dare both felt that they had only just dropped off to sleep when the bugle called them back to the cold world of men and war. The British troops were making an early start, and before the sun was over the tree-tops, the men were in the saddle and once more on the trail of their prey. The day promised to be a hot one before the sun was very high, and the troops were thankful when the road led them through brief snatches of woodland, for the shade was very grateful.

They rode onward until about ten that morning, when suddenly the leaders, who were keeping a sharp lookout for signs of the fugitives, came to an abrupt halt. The road led close to the water's edge here, and something that they had seen was evidently of great interest.

"Must have found a trail or some sign of the men you are after," Tom said to one of the soldiers. "I suppose if you catch those fellows Tim and I can leave you."

"I don't know, but I guess the major won't hold you any longer if we have the other parties in our hands. What do you want to hurry away from us for anyhow?"

"We're bound north and you fellows don't seem to be going that way," Tom replied, being careful to say nothing that would make the British soldiers suspicious.

"Sure and Oi wouldn't moind travelling a bit with you, if it wasn't for the awful hours you're keepin'," said Tim, yawning. "You keep us all up all night with good stories aginst which Oi have nothing, but to rout a man from his bed of roses at such an hour as we were this very morning is positively indacent."

"There go the officers," said the trooper on their right, as the little group rode past. They had been following in the company's rear, but the halt told them that something had happened up front and they were galloping up to investigate. The bright uniforms and well-fed forms impressed Tom with the great difference between these well-paid soldiers of a foreign monarch and his own struggling friends.

"They make a pretty sight," he said, half to himself.

"Why don't you join the regiment then?" asked one of the soldiers, who was paid a commission for securing recruits. "We all have a chance to rise, you know, and a couple of likely young fellows like yourselves ought to get along rapidly.

"But if we joined," said Tim, "and ever fell into the other side's clutches, then where would we be?"

"And with such capable men above us as yourself our promotion would, I'm afraid, be slow," Tom added, diplomatically.

The ambitious Britisher was too much flattered by this last remark to have any good reply ready, and before he could think up any new reasons, word ran down the column to move forward.

"They may have found a trail," said a Redcoat as the news sifted back through the ranks.

"Just the two of them?" queried a comrade. "I'm surprised that they found it."

"No, seems that there are a lot of Indians in this party, but the scouts seem to make out the foot-prints of two men who had shoes on."

"That's the pair, I'll wager," said a third. "That is how they got away from us yesterday, found some friendly Indians to take them away in canoes. No wonder we couldn't find their track."

Tom made no comment, but he gave Tim a knowing wink which so distracted that worthy's attention that an accident was only barely avoided.

"This is foine ridin'," said Tim, as a branch of a tree nearly took him out of his saddle. "Why the divil don't those two people you're devotin' your young lives to chasin' keep on good roads and not go trappin' it off into these woods?"

"If we have to chase them far we'll show you some fine places," said the soldier who had told the story the night before.

"Those two led us some pretty chases back on the old roads, and from the looks of this log track we're following, we'll be getting into worse ones before long."

"And a foine time we'll be havin' getting back to New York, or even Philadelphia for that matter, after we have been keepin' you company in these wild wanderings ages upon ages," Tim complained.

"Don't blame us for it," answered his soldier friend, "it's the officer's doings you know, not ours."

"Look out, Tim!" yelled Tom Dare suddenly, as the trooper's horse ahead of the Irish boy shied violently and rose so high on its hind legs that it almost seemed that both horse and rider would topple over backwards.

"Faith, and what's the trouble with ye?" queried Tim, indignantly, of the man ahead.

"Don't know," replied he, trying to appear calm, but really very much alarmed. "This nag must have seen a ghost."

"There it goes," shouted Tom, leaping quickly from his saddle and darting into the underbrush. "Come here, quick, some of you. I haven't any gun or sword, or even a stick."

Two or three of the men followed him and hastily stepped aside as a huge rattler turned with waving head and darting fangs in their direction.

"Let's have your gun," said Tom, quickly reaching out his hand for the weapon nearest him. The soldier handed it over and retreated to a safer spot, out of reach of the threatening reptile.

Tom took careful aim and pulled the trigger. At the same instant he jumped back out of reach, but he was safe where he had stood. The shot, fired so close to the mark, had fairly blown off the head of the dangerous snake, and the soldiers gave a hearty round of applause at this excellent exhibition of marksmanship, for with a swaying, venomous snake before one, it is most difficult to fire true the first time.

"Good shot, young fellow," said the recruiting sergeant, heartily. "I'll ask the major if he doesn't think you could be trusted with a rifle, for a man like yourself would be a valuable addition to our ranks."

"Thanks," said Tom, hopefully, for he certainly would like to succeed in getting a rifle. He could see that the recruiter was still hopeful of enlisting the boys.

"And sure, if you trust thot boy with a gun, Oi'm to be gettin' wan at the same instant," said Tim. "You should see the rattles off the hundreds of snakes Oi mesilf have kilt intirely yet."

Tim said this with a broad grin on his face and the soldiers could not help laughing at his remarks. The sergeant, however, saw that Tim really wanted a gun if Tom got one, so he promised to do his best for both of them.

The log road that they had been following now was reduced to the roughest kind of a mountain trail, and their progress was greatly impeded. It was soon evident to the officers and men that the wagon with their supplies could never be brought along this trail, and in fact the horses seemed to be more trouble than they were worth.

"We'll have to dismount and finish this pursuit on foot," said the major, finally. "The trail is very recent and our men cannot be very far away."

"If we hurry at this stage of the game," said one of the junior officers, "we ought to be close to them soon, and it may save us endless days of pursuit."

"Then let's be quick about things," said the major, sharply. "You, Captain Schafer, return to Richmond and await us there. Take ten men, all the horses, and our utility wagon. We may catch these men in a day or two, so wait for four days at the foot of this hill, where the brook crosses the roadway. Then if we get our men and strike the back trail quickly, we'll have our mounts and won't have to foot it all the way home. Don't delay after four days, however, for the country is full of roving bands of traitors and rebels and we can't afford to risk all these horses any longer. Your responsibility is a heavy one, captain, but I am sure you will fulfill it with all care and diligence."

The captain saluted and said: "I'd like to go on with you, major, and round up those young rascals in a hurry, but I expect to see you back at the end, or before the end of four days, and the best of luck to all in your pursuit."

The men, at orders from their various superiors, dismounted and hurriedly gathered their blankets, canteens and weapons together, fastened their accoutrements in a roll and slung them on their backs. If there is anything a cavalry man dislikes, it is to be transformed into a foot soldier, and consequently there was some little grumbling amongst the men.

Tom, uncertain as to what party he was to go with, and rather undecided in his own mind as to which he wanted to stay with, walked forward to where the major was standing, superintending the actions of some of the troopers. Tim followed him, and suddenly grasped him by the shoulder.

"Try to stay with this bunch, Tom," he whispered. "We'll be able to do heaps and heaps of good for Dick, and we'll be after getting all the nearer to our journey's end."

"Good idea," said Tom, being decided by this argument to do his best to continue with the larger body of men.

"What's a good idea?" suddenly asked the young fellow whom Tom had noticed talking with the major when Tim and he were captured.

"We keep our good ideas for those who are able to appreciate them," replied Tom, for his first encounter with this youth had left him with no very pleasant feelings toward him.

"We'll see about that," said the other, advancing on Tom. "I'll teach you how to answer a gentleman when he speaks to you."

"When a gentleman speaks to me I'll know how to answer him," replied Tom, while Tim burst out laughing.

The added insult of Tim Murphy's laughter was too much for the hot blooded southerner, and he sprang at Tom with an arm upraised, intending to show the Dare boy who was master in this case. But Tom had had too many of such little frays to be caught napping, and quickly stepping aside, he stuck out his foot and pushed the furious boy as he plunged past him. Tim was standing directly behind where Tom Dare had been, and he grabbed the falling figure as he lost his balance with Tom's push.

"Saved your loife, me little man," said Tim, carelessly letting the young fellow slide prone upon the ground. He then turned and walked away with Tom toward the major.

"Ha, ha!" laughed the soldiers, greatly tickled to see the southerner get a tumble.

"You uns got a fall that time for sure," said one.

The indignant object of these remarks, however, was hastily brushing off clinging pine needles and dirt, and meanwhile hurrying up after his two intended victims.

The boys had reached the major and that officer was having difficulty in restraining his laughter, for although some distance away, he had seen the incident clearly.

Tom saluted and said, quickly: "My companion and I have gotten interested in this chase, and as it promises to last but a few days at the most, would like to go on with you rather than go back and await your return. We can't be set free, you say, until you capture whoever you are after, so we may as well try to help you out and hurry our freedom at the same time."

"Two burds at one stone," volunteered Tim, smilingly.

"These two fellows are up to something," interrupted the southerner, running up at that minute. "I heard one of them say that he had a good idea, so they must be planning to escape."

The major looked from the speaker to the two boys. They were smiling innocently.

"We had two good ideas, begging your pardon," explained Tom. "One we explained to this young man and the other one to you."

"They were both all right, I think," said the major. "And I think, as these boys are in my charge at the present time, Mr. Wilson, you had better leave them undisturbed in the future. It looks as if it would be better for both of you."

"But," sputtered the excited fellow, "they insulted me, they——"

"We'll discuss that at another time," said the officer, coldly. "You may go now," he added, turning to the boys.

They withdrew and returned to the busy camp of soldiers who inquired how the "old man" had taken the affair. All expressed their pleasure at the way the boys had handled the arrogant young civilian.

"Evidently," Tom said to Tim, "that fellow hasn't made himself popular with the men."

"Nor would I, mesilf, already yet," replied Tim, "if it wasn't to our very bist interists."

"Well, we'll have to make the best of it for awhile," returned Tom. "We'll do more good right here than anywhere else I can think of."

The men had by this time finished their arrangements, and with some parting jokes and laughing remarks the ten selected men who were to take the back trail strung out the horses in line and leading and driving them at the same time were soon out of sight winding along the twisting log road. Only the sound of their shouts to the horses and the crashing in the underbrush could be heard and finally even that grew fainter and died away in the distance.

The remainder of the company, some fifty-odd men and the officers, gathered up their burdens and arms, fell into place two by two and were soon strung out over a hundred yards of rough mountain trail.

"We are after them in earnest, now," said Tom Dare, softly, "and no matter what happens, Tim, old man, don't let them find us out and don't let them ever get near enough to Dick and Fritz to capture them."

"Thot's a foine little job for us two in this crowd," said Tim, "but we'll do our very best and it won't be our own fault at all, at all, if anything goes wrong."

"Things are going to go right," concluded Tom, "I feel it in my bones."

CHAPTER XII
THE NIGHT ATTACK.

Long before the sun had cast its rays on the tree tops, the Indian encampment was astir. The sky was just beginning to grow grey with the coming dawn when the hasty morning meal had been finished and the fires stamped out. The Indians also had seen the camp fires of their enemies across the bay, and they took especial pains in the morning to keep their blazes small and hidden in the slight hollows. Silently the two white boys and their red companions stole to the water's edge, launched their birch canoes and paddled away from their temporary camp. A heavy mist hung over the water and they wished to be well along before the sun's warm rays dispelled the blanket that hid them.

"It feels good to be able to paddle," said Dick.

The party in Fritz's canoe was right along side of his and the boys were able to keep up a quiet conversation at the start.

"Ve would by now be half to death frozen already," replied the Dutch boy, plying his paddle vigorously.

"Let's put a little energy into our strokes," suggested Dick. "We'll try to get up in the lead and keep the pace up."

"I am already pushing so fast as I can," replied Fritz.

"Then we'll leave you at the tail end in about five minutes," said Dick, as he dug his paddle blade deep into the water and sent the frail canoe ahead by leaps and bounds. The Indians in Dick's canoe caught the idea at once, and although Fritz and his companions started right after them, they were not able to catch up. Dick soon was parallel with the chief's canoe and here his companions stopped paddling and looked at Telca for instructions.

"Ve haf caught you so soon," panted Fritz, drawing up abreast at that moment.

"You never would have if we hadn't stopped so as not to lose you," answered Dick.

"Sometimes you are right, not, and this is it," said Fritz.

"Which way now, chief?" asked Dick of the Indian.

"You can follow Telca," said he, and speaking to his bow companion, the chief suddenly drove his own craft out ahead of the others and with a quick succession of powerful strokes was soon several lengths in the lead.

Dick Dare and his party were soon after the flying leaders, but the chief and his paddling mate were well matched, and strain as they might, the others could do no more than hold their own, and never gained a foot. If they had started to overtake Telca, he could undoubtedly have drawn away from them with a little added effort, for the two in the foremost canoe seemed not to be exerting themselves to their fullest.

Half an hour's paddling of this kind brought the leaders almost over to the other shore, and some distance further to the West. The chief now ceased paddling entirely and held his shining blade in the air as a sign for the others to slow up with him. Their nearness to the shore made silence necessary, and when the sternmost craft had come up, they all moved forward very cautiously.

"That was warm work," said Dick quietly. "The chief can certainly give us lessons in paddling."

"Another half minute and I surely haf been a deader," replied Fritz. "Such vork I nefer did yet, in veeks before."

Keeping close to the shore, the little flotilla went onward until they reached a small brook opening into the bay. Here they could see the narrow road running close to the water's edge.

"We land here," ordered Telca, turning his canoe toward the bank.

"What are you going to do with the canoes?" asked Dick. "It seems a shame to destroy them."

"We will all get out except four of the young men," said Telca. "They will tow the birch boats to the land out there, and we will send word to our brothers, the Delawares, where the Redman has hidden them. They may have them, for they were our friends when we came across the mountains twelve moons ago."

"I'm glad they are not going to be wasted. They are such beauties," Dick said. "And that idea of having us all go ashore here and hiding them around the peninsular is a fine one."

The Indians quickly stepped out, gathered up their few possessions and their rifles, and roped the canoes together so that the four young men whom Telca had picked out might convey the whole string to the hiding place.

"Young men catch up to us soon," volunteered Telca. "We will not wait."

"Hope they do," replied Dick. "We aren't any too strong now and every man will count if we run into that British troop again."

"Young men will be with their people by the end of this sun," responded Telca, confidently. "Young men travel fast."

"Mein gootness, I'm glat ve don'd haf to race like those fellars," said Fritz. "Und also I could vish Tim Murphies vas mit dem."

"Why?" asked Dick.

"Dot Irisher, I vould haf his legs run off alreaty," chuckled Fritz.

"I wish we knew for certain where he and Tom are," replied Dick.

"Berhabs they vould call on us this efening," said Fritz.

"Well, wondering won't do any good, so let's move along. The tribe are striking off along the trail, and if we want to go with them at all we had better hurry. These Indians are awful fast travelers when they want to be."

Dick and Fritz picked up the rifles they had borrowed from the Indians and set off after the party. The pace was swift and they were soon in the rougher and less traveled trails. The red men moved without any apparent effort and glided noiselessly along, yet covering the ground in very quick time. The women, although carrying light burdens, were just as accustomed to the trail as their masters, and made no complaint as they followed their leaders.

"If I should von of those red wimmins marry, yet, I vould do no more vork already," said Fritz.

"And I just hope that if you get anyone to take care of you for the rest of your life, that it's one of the kind that keeps you moving," replied Dick, laughing.

"Dot's just my luck wot is, to got von like it," grumbled Fritz.

"This is sure enough a rough path," said Dick, as they stumbled over the roots of a giant tree that stretched across the trail.

"Yah, this is for roughness a vonder," replied Fritz.

In spite of the difficulties of the trail, however, the band made exceptionally rapid progress and with but a brief halt at noon-day for a hasty meal and a short breathing space, they pushed on again and by nightfall were far into the mountains.

That evening Dick asked Telca about the four young men whom they had left with the canoes.

"They will sleep with us before the next sun," replied the chief.

Dick didn't say any more on that subject, but he was still wondering where they were and whether or not they would have come across any trace of the pursuing party when he dropped off to sleep. Fritz had already fallen fast asleep and with the exception of the three solitary outposts, all were resting after their hard march.

A peaceful silence settled on the camp and the little fire-embers burned low and were not replenished. Silently from the darkness came the little woods creatures and gazed with black snapping eyes at the invaders of their forest home. Even the sentinels grew drowsy and had to change their positions to keep from falling asleep.

Then of a sudden all the little feathered and furred folk vanished into the wood. The Indian outposts crouched silently behind protecting trees, and then ran to the sleeping camp and hurriedly awakened it. A shot and then another had come to their ears faintly, borne on the night wind from far down the valley. Even as they roused the tribe more firing could be heard, and Dick and Fritz, like their red comrades, hurried to grasp their weapons and prepare for trouble.

"I'll bet it's those four Indians in some sort of trouble with the British," said Dick, remembering his thoughts of earlier in the evening. "Your young men, isn't it, chief?" he asked of Telca.

"Not know," responded that Indian, looking rather anxious about the matter, however. "Indian find out soon."

"We'll be with you while you are finding out, then," said Dick.

"Yah, I will be finding oud who has been shots firing into mein sleep yet," Fritz added.

The men of the tribe all filed off into the darkness, following Telca's lead, and Dick and the German boy followed. With all their knowledge and experience in wood-craft, the two Patriots found it difficult to keep up with the running Indians, but they managed to hold their own, although Fritz grunted considerably when he fell over an old log in his path.

Suddenly the men in the front halted and gathered about in a circle. Dick, coming up behind them, saw that they were grouped about three half-naked Indians whom he took to be the young men they had left behind. Evidently one of them was missing. The Indians were talking excitedly in quick, sharp sentences, and Dick gathered that they had come upon the Redcoat camp, taken a few shots at the pickets, and in the running fight that had followed one of them had fallen and had been overtaken before they could help him. They were uncertain as to whether their comrade had been wounded or had been overpowered. At any rate he was now a prisoner in the camp of their enemies, and even the older men counselled an attempt at rescue. They were eager to be avenged on their ancient enemies.

"We will bring our brother back with us. Let us remember our little sister also," said Telca.

"Ve haf no love lost on those Britisher fellows, too," said Fritz. "A few shoots vill berhabs stop their chasing us the whole vorld ofer."

"If you see two white boys in camp without uniforms, that is, Redcoats, don't fire at them," said Dick to the Indians. "They may be our brothers, held by the red coats as prisoners."

Telca communicated this to the warriors, and again they spread out and moved swiftly through the black forests. Here and there, little natural glades let in the starlight, and helped them to follow each other, but for the most part, all was inky darkness around them.

Almost before he expected it, Dick saw the twinkling fire lights of the English camp below them. Their pace decreased to a more careful one, and the whole party spread out into a fan shape, without any orders, each man his own general, as is the Indian custom.

Dick and Fritz were far to the right and they began a stealthy approach toward the British. Their comrades were soon hidden from view, except for Telca, who kept near them. They had drawn close to the line that should have marked the posts of the British pickets when Dick, Fritz and Telca caught the sound of a voice close at hand. No figures was visible, which afterward proved to be an important thing, but nevertheless, the three paused and listened intently. Telca finally motioned the boys to creep forward again. They were all mystified about the lack of soldiers about the fires in the distance. The blazes burned brightly, but no forms showed between them and the silent red-men. Suddenly from the other side of the circle came the call of a night bird, and the tribe knew that the other end of the line had reached their position. When Telca answered that call the fight was to begin. But the chief never had to answer it. The sound of the bird call had just died away into silence when a voice near the little group said softly in a rich Irish accent,

"Faith and it's stiff Oi'm afther gettin' to be. If———"

"Tim! Tom!" called Dick, quietly.

But he had spoken too soon. There was a British soldier with Tom and Tim, and behind them, about twenty yards, were a full row of men lying in wait for just such an attack as was threatening them.

The English trooper leaped to his feet and fired his rifle directly at the spot from whence came Dick's voice. In the darkness the shot fortunately went wild, but the alarm had been given and the battle was on.

Telca, taking careful aim, dropped the soldier where he stood and Tom and Tim, firing their guns wildly over their heads, dashed off into the woods away from Dick and his companions. They hoped by so doing to get out of the way of the bullets from the British behind them, and also lead the oncoming troopers astray as to Dick's position, for Tom feared that Dick and Fritz might be alone and therefore might be captured.

The two boys were far from being alone, however, as the whole British force soon discovered. The woods around them became a mass of shooting tongues of flame, and the sharp fire of the attacking Indians soon forced the Redcoats to take shelter behind the trees and rocks. For a full half hour the Indians circled about the cordon of troops, firing and yelling and making the night fiendish with their blood-curdling cries. Several of the English, more exposed because of the fires burning behind them, fell, wounded or killed. But their numbers were too great for the redskins to overcome and they were gradually driven back at various points and finally forced to cease firing and retire in the darkness. The fight had been brisk while it lasted and several times it looked as if the Indians might break the defence and complete their victory. But in the end, the greater numbers of the British succeeded in repulsing the attack, and with the loss of one man and several slightly wounded, the Indians retired into the forest, abandoning the attempt to rescue their captive brother.

"Vas has happened to dot Tom und Tim Murphies?" queried Fritz as they hurried back to the Indian encampment. "Dot fool Irisher ran the woods off in, like the crazy feller he iss, und Tom vas following him after."

"They saved you and Telca and I by doing it," replied Dick. "It certainly led the British astray for a minute."

"Maype Tim has some senses after all, alreaty," said Fritz, thoughtfully. "I vould nefer tell him so yet."

"Well, they seem to be in all right with the British and we can always hope to be warned, at least, if we get into danger."

"Und now, vere are ve going at?" asked the Dutch boy as they reached camp and found the squaws ready to move on.

"Going to march some more," replied the chief. "Redcoat man too near."

Fritz gave a longing glance at his heap of pine boughs, where he had hoped to pass the rest of the night, shouldered his gun, and trudged off with a sigh after Dick.

CHAPTER XIII
THE CLIFF DROP.

Tom Dare and Tim returned somewhat slowly to the camp after the firing had ceased, and the Indians had retired from the attack.

"It's hard to see any man shot down before your eyes," said Tom, "but it's a good thing for you and I, Tim, that the trooper that heard Dick call us by name isn't here to tell the story."

"Sure, if he was, it's you and I, me bye, would now be chasin' the woods through trying to foind that brother of yours and his rid skinned frinds."

"Come along, we'll go report to the major, and see where we stand," said Tom.

"Good," replied Tim, "Do you know, Tom, it's a lucky thing for us, it is, thot with thot crazy Dootchman firin' at us we wern't kilt entirely."

"Careful, Tim, don't talk too much with these men around. They might overhear something."

The two boys had reached the major by now, and going up to him, saluted. Tim said that saluting a British major was the hardest work he had ever done in his short but eventful life.

The major was plainly upset by the loss his troops had suffered, but he evidently did not suspect the boys of anything wrong, for he smiled gravely when he saw them, and merely said, "There will be plenty of room in the troop for you two now, I think. We have driven off those red-skinned devils, but it has cost us pretty dearly. You two gave the first alarm, didn't you?"

"I think we were the first to discover the enemy," replied Tom, quietly.

"Good," returned the officer, "I shall remember your services."

When they had withdrawn, Tim had great difficulty in restraining his laughter, but they soon had to turn and help the wounded troopers, which effectually drove all thoughts of mirth out of the boys' minds.

The wounded men were made as comfortable as possible, and it was decided to dispatch a messenger to the ten troopers who had been sent down with the horses, to come up and convey them back to the nearest settlement for further care.

The dead were to be buried in the morning, and it was almost daybreak when the tired soldiers and Tom and Tim finally turned in to snatch a hasty nap. They threw out an ample picket line and waited for morning to take up the pursuit again.

Early on the morrow the camp was all astir, and before taking up the trail again, a council of war was held, and it was decided to execute the Indian prisoner, whose capture had brought about the attack, as a lesson to the redmen.

Tom heard of this brutal plan, and resolved to see what he could do to upset the arrangements. He and Tim talked it over, but could arrive at no safe way to set the Indian free. Any friendly move on their part would have brought trouble upon their own heads, and they were still seeking for a feasible scheme when the company took up the march, the Indian in their midst, with his hands tied behind him.

"Ividently they are not going to have the hanging hereabouts," said Tim.

"No, they must be hard to suit," replied Tom. "There are dozens of big trees all around, and yet there are none that please them."

"Oi have an oidea that it's some showy place the villains are afther."

"Probably," agreed Tom. "They want to make an example so that every Indian that goes through these forsaken parts can see."

"Hi there, boys, the major wants you back at the end of the line," called a trooper to Tim and Tom, just then.

"All right," responded Tom, as they turned to obey the summons.

"Phat can the ould feller be afther?" queried Tim.

"Don't know," answered Tom. "But we'll see in a minute."

The major was walking rapidly along behind the first company of men, and by his side the young southerner, who had been in turn so antagonistic to each of the Dare boys.

"There is a very serious charge against you, young men," said the officer. "Mr. Andrews, here, says you are friends of the party we are after, and that during the fight last night you communicated with them. What have you to say?"

"Evidently, Mr. Andrews has been misinformed, for we held no communication with the enemy last night, and I hoped that we had proved our loyalty before you to your cause, by our actions," replied Tom, looking the young civilian up and down while he was speaking, as if he was some object of curiosity.

"I thought myself that you were all right, last night, but it seems that no one remembers seeing you after the first alarm until the fighting was over, and that fact, together with Mr. Andrews' suspicions, and the further fact that you were with us under rather peculiar circumstances, forces me to put you to the test."

The major paused here, and both the boys wondered what sort of test the trial was to be.

"Well, foire ahead," said Tim, impatiently, "we are here because you keep us, and thin you are afther doubtin' our wantin' to be with ye."

"If you are with us as spies, and are friendly with the other party, you know the penalty, of course," said the officer, sternly. "We propose to hang the Indian prisoner this morning, if we reach the proper place before noon, and that execution will give you a good chance to prove yourselves. You are to be the ones to carry out the sentence!"

Tom was dumfounded. They meant to make Tim and himself commit the murder, for that was what it would amount to, of one of their own allies, one of the men who had helped Dick and Fritz. The idea was a shrewd one on the part of the British.

Tim, however, instead of being upset by the idea, merely grew angry.

"Faith, an' out of two respictable, quiet citizens, you would be makin' us to be your executioners, would ye?" he questioned angrily.

The major shrugged his shoulders.

"Look at it as you like, my man," he replied. "If you are with us it won't be hard, and if you are against us, well you can take your choice."

Yes, that was just it. They had planned as nice a trap for the two boys as could be invented. Tom felt tempted to blow out the major's brains where he stood and take their chances in the woods. But the odds were too great even for his daring spirit, and the Indian would be still in the same position as he was now in.

"We must give that matter a little thought," said Tom, finally. "Even in our position as members of this troop, we need to get accustomed to our task, and if we may talk it over for a few minutes we may be able to reconcile ourselves to our disagreeable duty."

"You haven't much time," said the major, shortly. "We may come to our selected place any minute, now, so be quick, and you had better turn over your guns to the corporal in the meantime. After you have proven yourselves worthy you can have them back, and we will admit you in full standing to the troop."

As they turned away there was a sneer on the face of the young southerner, and Tom felt doubly anxious to beat out their enemies on that account, for he had grown to cordially dislike the young civilian.

"Sure, an' we seem to be up against it, intirely," said Tim, gloomily. "We can't hang the poor divil of an Injin, an' if we don't there'll be no more of the likes of us around much longer, whatever."

"We have got to figure some way out of this," Tom said, firmly. "Have you any weapons about you?"

"Weapons is it?" asked Tim. "If ye can call this foldin' knife a weapon, ye'll be doin' well."

"It may be better than nothing," said Tom. "Try to keep it, anyhow, and don't let anyone see it again."

"Where is it they are so anxious to hold their entertainmint?" asked Tim.

"I don't know. We'll ask some of the men," answered Tom.

"Ask the corporal," said the first trooper they questioned. "He has been through here before, and it's him as has picked out the spot."

The boys went forward to find the corporal. They came up to him, near the head of the line.

"Where is it we are going to string up the Indian?" asked Tom, indifferently.

"Oh, it's a great place for a sign like that to hang," replied the corporal. "There is a big bare tree, I think it's a cedar, and it's right on top of a rocky mountain's back. The trail we are following leads right up to it, and the only other trail around here runs———"

"The major wants you at once!" a soldier ran up and interrupted them just at that point.

"Runs where?" said Tom, eagerly.

"I will tell you when you come back from the major. We are most there now, so you will see for yourself soon."

"So there is another trail, Tim," said Tom, excitedly. "And to think that we almost got a description of it, and then we are sent for. Well, we'll tell that old fox of a major that we'll obey his commands under protest, and run our chances of———"

"If it don't rain, it'll be a foine day, Oi'm thinkin'," said Tim, cutting short Tom's comment and plans as the young southerner came into sight.

"Do you know, Tom, there are some parties, mentionin' no names, moind ye, that are certainly very nosy around these parts."

"And I'm thinkin', my young rebel, that there'll be two young spies less 'nosey' before a great while," rejoined the youth. "For one, I shall be glad to see the end of you."

"Phat a happy party it would be with anither wan loike you about," replied Tim, looking for further trouble with their enemy.

But the youth chose to ignore him, and hurried on to the major, with the two boys following.

"Well," asked the officer, when they had come up, "what have you decided?"

"There wasn't much to decide," replied Tom. "We shall have to obey your orders, but we shall do so under protest, and shall report the matter to the representatives of the crown when we get back to Philadelphia."

"I represent His Majesty, here," said the major, "and your complaints will do no good. We are, I understand, approaching the spot which has been selected for you to perform your duty in, and you will soon be called upon to do your part and prove your assertion that you are not spies."

"We'll do our part," said Tom, grimly, and thought at the same time that perhaps that part would be a counter surprise to the major.

The morning was well advanced before they finally came to a sharp rise in the trail, and after a half hour of climbing, they reached the summit of the ridge. The party ahead of them seemed to have scattered where the trail began to rise, and they were unable to find any trace of them on the upper ridge of the mountain.

The great tree that had probably served before in the same gruesome office for which it was selected to-day, stood bare and forbidding against the sky line.

There didn't seem to be anything but sky beyond the edge of the ridge, while the trail they were on ran just below the top, and along the back of the mountain. There certainly was no escape in that direction.

The troopers formed in a semi-circle to prevent any bolt for liberty, and the two boys walked forward with the Indian between them. His hands were still tied behind his back, and of the entire party, the redman seemed to be the least affected. He was prepared to accept his fate with the calm stoicism of his race.

"If we cut your ropes, can we escape?" inquired Tom, softly, as they drew near the tree.

The Indian's eyes glinted responsively, and he nodded his head affirmatively.

"How?" asked Tom, pretending to fix the rope which was supposed to swing the Indian off his feet.

"Over the cliff edge. Roll down," replied the Redman.

Tom glanced up at the branches of the tree, apparently selecting one over which to throw the rope. In reality he was looking over the side of the cliff, and it was not an encouraging view. There was what looked like a straight drop of a hundred feet before he saw a ledge, and further down in the valley he could make out the glitter of a tiny stream, rushing down through the valley.

"Hurry up, there," called an authoritative voice from the half circle of troopers.

"All ready," called back Tom. Then in a whisper, he said, "Out with your knife, Tim and slice those wrist cords, and when I throw the end of this rope up into the tree, over the edge we must go. Relax your muscles and drop. Understand?" he asked, turning to the Indian.

"Ugh, good," he replied.

Tim stepped behind the redskin, and with one strong pull, severed the rope about his wrists. The Indian never moved his arms to indicate to the others what had been done, and at that minute Tom hurled the end of the rope high into the air, and instantly dropped over the edge of the cliff.

The other two followed on Tom Dare's heels, and a volley rang out almost coincidently.

CHAPTER XIV
EVADING THE ENEMY.

The Indian party, with Dick and Fritz, reached a point where the trails divided early that morning. With the coming of daylight their spirits rose, and the encounter of the previous night took on a more encouraging aspect. They had undoubtedly caused considerable loss to the company of British, and had escaped with but few wounds themselves. Telca was anxious to trap the Redcoats in some deep gorge, where the Indians would have the pursuing party at their mercy, and was hurrying on so as to keep out of the reach of their antagonists until the right moment should arrive. Dick and Fritz were anxious to reach the Ohio river near Fort Pitt, for there they hoped to get canoes to carry them down the river to a point directly south of Vincennes. Here Dick proposed to strike off through a forest trail and then travel north again to their final destination.

"Which way do we go now?" asked Dick of the chief.

"The bottom road," replied Telca. "All spread out here," he commanded, "we go up part way, come down again, so," and he showed the boys how they were to climb some distance up alongside of the trail and descend backwards so that the footprints would all point toward the top. By scattering over a wide space they would lead the British into thinking that they had decided to take to the upper path and had scattered to hide their trail, and by edging toward the right when they descended they would be able to come down on the branch track around the spur of the mountain and follow that to the end of the valley.

They hoped to make the mouth of the valley by nightfall, and if the British stuck to the upper trail, they would gain some distance unmolested.

"I hope this little stunt works," said Dick, as they scrambled down the steep mountain side, holding sometimes with their hands and at others slipping and clutching at rocks and bushes.

"Yah, mit all this troubles, it should some goot do yet, for sure," replied Fritz. "I have no more skin my hands on alreatty."

"Go right on and wear out the bones, then," laughed Dick. "You have got to get down some way."

There was a sudden slipping and sliding beside him, and before Dick could save himself, Fritz had grasped him by the heels in a vain effort to maintain his position and they both ended in a cloud of dirt and leaves at the bottom of the descent.

"For why don't you hold on, und not push me to the bottoms?" asked Fritz, digging the dirt out of one eye.

"You crazy Dutchman," said Dick. "I'll have to leave you home until you learn how to stand up after this."

"Such an unreasonable feller," sighed Fritz, resignedly. "Always I should got plamed for dings."

"If you don't get up and brush yourself off," said Dick, "the dust cloud will still be floating around here when that British party catches up."

The mention of the English troops spurred Fritz into action, and he hastily gathered himself together and was ready to go ahead again.

Most of the Indian tribe were already far along the trail, and the boys had to hurry and catch up to them. The day proved a long one for the two Patriots for the sun was hot in the valley, and they were pushed to the utmost to keep up to the Indian leaders. Except for a short halt now and then when they all drank from some nearby rushing brook, they had been on the trail since before dawn. The men were also without any rest since the fight of the day before.

The signal from Telca that they were to make camp was a very welcome one.

"Well, I feel as if we had done a good day's work," said Dick, as they sat on a fallen log and watched the squaws gather wood for the fires.

"Och, Dick Dare, a veek of whole sleep vill not my feet rest yet," replied Fritz.

"See how small and how well concealed those squaws build their fires," said Dick. "Each one behind a tree or rock to keep anyone on that ridge up there from seeing the light."

"So soon yet as they got somedings cooked, I don'd care vhere they haf fires," Fritz returned.

In a surprisingly short time the food in the kettles was steaming, and the whole party felt strength returning to their tired muscles after eating and resting.

Telca joined the boys after having satisfied his appetite, and unfolded to them his plans for the immediate future. An hour's march further along the trail along the mountain ridge came down and joined the one they were following. Just beyond that was the "big water," as Telca called the river, where they would search for canoes for the boys. The Indians would wait for the British troops where the trails met, for there were high wooded rocky slopes on both sides of the fork, and the Redman would have a position of great advantage for an ambush.

"But wouldn't it be well to take up that position to-night?" asked Dick.

"Don'd please some more mofe yet to-night," said Fritz. "After to-day's valk ve should be py the Pacific Ocean already."

Telca considering Dick's suggestion, puffed deliberately at his pipe.

"The mountain path is shorter than valley one," said the Indian. "If soldiers walk all day, be most there to-night. Maybe go through before sun to-morrow."

"Then, let's get there to-night," said Dick. "You say it's an hour's tramp, and we can get there and take up our position before there is any possible chance of the British getting past."

"You right," finally said Telca. "We move on now."

"Ve don'd nefer sleep," grumbled Fritz, "und ven ve haf a chance, you must vent and spoil id."

"Well, we'll be back on the water soon, and you can let your legs sleep while you paddle with your arms," said Dick, laughing.

After gathering up their packs and putting out all the fires, the Indians started out for their final camp. It was pitch dark when they arrived at the selected place, and they all rolled up in their blankets wherever they could find a level space big enough to hold them. Three of the Redmen stalked away through the trees to keep watch over the sleeping tribe, and both Dick and Fritz were glad that they were not forced to take turns standing guard, after so long a day on the trail.

The next morning proved to be wet and rainy, and, although the Indians apparently did not object to the condition of the weather, the boys were both very uncomfortable. Their long campaigning, however, had taught them to make the best of everything. A careful investigation failed to disclose the whereabouts of the British troop, and Dick and Fritz finally decided to go ahead to the river bank, which was only a mile from where they had slept, and see what prospect there was of getting a canoe. One of the Indians accompanied them, and they hurried briskly down the trail through the fog.

They had almost reached the river's edge, when the Redman saw the glimmer of a fire through the mist and the trees. Crouching quickly, he pulled Dick and Fritz with him, and pointed in the direction of the blaze.

Evidently the fire was but just started and not burning strongly as yet, for it would flare up and die down as a breeze encouraged it or the dampness retarded it.

"Indian," whispered the companion.

"How do you know?" asked Dick, searching about him for some sign of life.

The redskin pointed to the faint track of two moccasined feet, both exactly parallel with each other.

"White man no walk like that," said their companion.

"Wonder if they're friends or foes?" whispered Dick to Fritz.

The Dutch boy's teeth chattered with the cold when he started to talk, but the Indian motioned for them to be silent.

"Come," he said, leading the way into some long wet grass. Wriggling carefully along on their stomachs, the three made a detour about the spot where they figured the camp to be. The Indian left them for a few moments and approached nearer to the fire. In a moment he was back again.

"No good Indian," he said, in a low voice. "Not friend of Telca's people. Not friend of white boy."

"How many?" questioned Dick.

The Indian held up both hands to indicate that he had counted ten figures in the Indian camp.

"Canoe on shore," he added in a whisper.

"Only one?" asked Dick, in surprise.

"Five canoe," replied the Indian.

"If we can only get one," said Dick, "we'll be fixed for several days to come."

Just then the sound of a volley of musketry came to their ears.

"Mein gootness, what is dot?" said Fritz, excitedly.

"The British," whispered Dick. "It's firing from the valley. The troopers have evidently caught up to our friends."

"Dose oder red-fellers has heard, too," said Fritz.

The three in the grass peered anxiously at the hazy group about the strange camp fire.

"Me go back," said their Indian companion, suddenly. "Tell Telca enemy here. White boy get canoe. Good-bye."

He held out a dark hand to Fritz and Dick, and squeezed each of their hands.

"Tell Telca good-bye," said Dick. "White boys never forget Indian's friendship."

The Indian nodded, and turning, crawled off through the grass toward the shelter of the woods beyond the trail. The firing had grown more brisk from the rear, and although they were so far away, the boys could hear the loud roll of the British firing line, and the occasional barks of the Redskins' rifles.

Suddenly out of the mist near them, the new Indian party emerged, running warily toward the sound of the fight. Dick and Fritz ducked down into the grass just in time to save discovery. The ten Redskins filed past toward the trail, and when they were almost out of sight the two patriots began to move cautiously toward the deserted camp. The fire was smoking and smouldering, and on the shore were five canoes, all of bark, drawn up clear of the water and inverted to keep them dry inside.

"Fine," ejaculated Dick. "There doesn't seem to be any difference in these canoes, Fritz. Grab hold of that end and we'll slide her into the stream."

"You such a robber are I vill pe afraid to stay py you again," said Fritz.

"All's fair in war, you know," replied Dick.

"Couldn't ve py any possibility take all five mit us?" asked Fritz.

"Now, who's the robber?" laughed Dick. "But come on, you old turn about. We can't lose a minute now. Stick the end of your gun through the bottom of that boat."

"But dot vill spoilt it," remonstrated Fritz.

"That's just what I want it to do," said Dick, jabbing his gun through the frail craft nearest him.

Fritz poked the muzzle of his rifle through the bottom of another one, but in withdrawing it accidentally pulled the trigger.

"Och, oh!" he yelled.

"Fritz!" said Dick, sharply. "Have you hurt yourself?"

"Nein, I don'd guess so," replied the German boy.

"Good, for that at least," said Dick, thankfully. "Come on now, those fellows will be back here in a shake after all that racket."

The two boys hurriedly grasped the ends of the canoe, shoved it into the river and stepped into their new craft.

"Paddle for your life!" called Dick, from the stern.

"Yah," said Fritz, "I am alreatty."

They had only gotten about a hundred yards out into the stream when the boys heard an exclamation from the shore. Turning, Dick saw the Indians file out of the woods, and reach the canoes. Two of them started to launch one of the boats, while the others aimed their guns at Dick and Fritz.

"Duck, duck down," called Dick, and as they did so, the rifles of the angry redskins barked out. One bullet splashed in the water near the canoe, and the rest whistled uncomfortably over their heads. The two Indians had gotten one of the damaged canoes into the water, but as they stepped into it, it began to fill through the rent in the bottom.

Dick leaned down, dropped his paddle and took up his rifle.

"Keep on paddling, Fritz," he said, quietly. "I'll take a chance of hitting one of those red fellows."

Dick's rifle cracked, and one of the Redmen gave a cry of pain and surprise, put his hand over his left shoulder, and staggered backwards. The others turned and sought shelter behind rocks while they reloaded their guns, which gave the boys additional time to increase the distance between them.

They were now near the further shore, and when the Indians fired again, their bullets flew wild, leaving the boys unharmed.

"Run right ashore," said Dick. "We'll carry this canoe with us for a ways and launch it again further down stream. The mist is rising, so we've got to hurry if we want to get away from those fellows without being seen."

CHAPTER XV
UNITED.

A week had passed since Dick Dare and Fritz made their escape from the Indians. They had paddled steadily down the river, and by making their night stops short and their day trips long, they had almost reached the point where they were to leave the canoes and take to the trail again.

"Guess we'll camp here to-night," said Dick, when it had grown so dark that further traveling was risky. "It looks like a good spot and we'll get an early start and try to reach the end of our river journey by to-morrow night."

Fritz breathed a sigh of relief.

"Yah," he said. "It looks already like a goot blace to sleep."

"Well, we are on the last stage of the trip now," said Dick, "and if we can keep up this pace we will get to Vincennes ahead of time."

"Vhere iss Tom und Tim Murphies, I vonder?" commented Fritz. "Ve shall be at Vinzennes pefore dhose two, I think it, yes, no?"

"I'm surprised that Tom and Tim haven't joined us before this," Dick said. "Perhaps they haven't fared very well in the British troop. They seemed to have their liberty, though, so I don't see why they shouldn't be right along behind us."

"Brobably it's dot Murphies feller is making troubles," Fritz suggested.

"You have a great idea of Tim, haven't you?" laughed Dick.

"He iss a all right feller, Tim iss, but he isn't a Deutcher," Fritz replied.

"I'll bet he feels bad about that," suggested Dick.

"Dot's chust the trouble, I don'd peliefe he does," Fritz answered seriously, much to Dick's amusement.

The boys paddled in to the shore, pulled the canoe out of the water, and after eating their supper proceeded to make themselves as comfortable as possible for the night.

"We better not light any fires," said Dick. "We had one this morning and I guess we can get along without it now."

"Look!" said Fritz, who was standing near the canoe at the water's edge. "Dot looks like somedings iss burning."

Dick joined him and gazed upstream in the direction that Fritz indicated toward the opposite shore.

"Seems to be a camp fire," said Dick. "Who can be camping there, I wonder?"

"Perhaps some Indians yet?" suggested Fritz.

"It must be," agreed Dick. "We better pull this canoe further in, for if they go down the river before us in the morning they might spot it. Maybe it's those fellows we got this canoe from."

"We had better be careful, then," said Fritz. "If dhose felers efer caughted us, ve vould a bad time have."

"Guess we'll have to keep watch to-night," Dick answered. "You turn in now, Fritz, and I'll wake you up in about four hours. Then you can give me a chance to snatch a nap. We can't afford to take chances, you know."

"Don'd forget to call me," replied Fritz, with a grin.

With this quite needless admonition the Dutch boy rolled up in his blanket and Dick soon had evidence from his heavy breathing that he was fast asleep.

Dick felt very drowsy, and after walking down to the shore and back again several times to keep awake, he decided that the more practical thing to do was to slide the canoe into the water and investigate the camp on the point higher up the river. Fritz, he knew, would sleep for a week, if he were not disturbed, so Dick decided to improve him time by finding out, if possible, who his neighbors were.

He paddled quietly, hugging the shore to within a hundred yards of the point where the fire had been seen, and then headed for the spot. There was no sign of life about the fire, as far as Dick could tell, and he judged the strangers must be sleeping. The canoe was now very close to the river bank and because of the darkness, Dick did not discover the little shoal of pebbles before him until the canoe grated on them with quite a little noise.

Dick sat perfectly motionless for several minutes. He was hoping that the sound had not carried to the ears of the other party. For an interval all was still, and then suddenly Dick heard a sound right beside him in the bushes at the water's edge.

He turned and was about to paddle quickly away when a figure stepped out of the woods with a gun pointed directly at the Dare Boy.

"One move, and we'll shoot!" said a voice from in front of him, and Dick saw a second figure in front of the canoe.

"Foine," said the first figure, "we've got him now, be jabbers."

"Tim, Tom!" cried Dick. "Don't you know who you have captured?"

"Be the powers, it's Dick Dare!" ejaculated Tim, while Tom dropped his gun and waved his hat in the air.

"Not so loud, Tim," said Dick. "There may be others within a hundred miles, you know, and if there are any they'll hear you. This is certainly great, though. I never thought it was your fire. I was just going to investigate."

Dick had pulled the bow of the canoe ashore and exchanged warm hand-clasps and many claps on the back with his brother and Tim.

"Come on down and we'll join Fritz," said Dick. "We are safer away from that fire of yours, anyhow."

"Same old Dick," said Tom. "Always take command as soon as there's anyone to boss."

"You and Tim have been bossing each other long enough by now," replied Dick, laughing. "You need some one to look after you for a change."

"Well, we've gotten as far along as you have," rejoined Tom.

"Excipt for a quater av a mile or so," commented Tim.

"That's right," replied Dick. "The honors are even, I guess."

The boys startled Fritz out of his sleep by their return to camp, and the scene that had occurred when Dick met the others was reenacted. Even Tim and Fritz were glad to see each other and buried their rivalry in the joy of being reunited.

"When did you leave the British troop?" asked Dick, finally.

"I better give an account of our trip right from the start, to get things straight," said Tom.

"It'll be an all night job if ye'll be tellin' all the advintures av us," protested Tim.

"Well, I'll just tell how we left the service of King George then," said Tom, laughing. He told then briefly of their experiences while with the English troops and how, just as they were supposed to prove their loyalty by hanging the Indian, all three of them had plunged over the edge of the cliff.

"It was a desperate chance, but by good luck we all landed on a ledge a little way down," said Tom.

"It's a wonder you were not all killed," said Dick.

"I thought sure our last hour had come," admitted Tim.

"Anyway," Tom went on, "our fall was pretty much broken by the bushes and various growths we tumbled through. When we got to our feet we hugged in close to the wall of rock that rose above and by our side and with the bushes overhead and a slight hollow in the ledge to hide us, the troopers never saw us at all."

"They think sure thot we are falling yet," put in Tim.

"I guess they believed that we had gone down clear to the bottom. Anyway, if we had, I don't think any of us would have ever lived to tell the tale. The Redcoats didn't stay looking for us long, and by noon-time we crawled out, then by slipping, sliding, holding fast and helping each other, we got down the rest of the mountain side and struck the lower trail that we had hoped to find."

"What happened then?" asked Dick, while Fritz sat with his mouth wide open to catch every detail.

"Well, next day we got down to a place where the trails meet again and there were a bunch of Indians holding a pow-pow, celebrating a victory over the same British troop from whom we had escaped the day before. Of course our Indian companion recognized them at once and insisted on our going with him."

"Sure, but they were a friendly lot, and we were mighty hungry by that time," said Tim.

"They were friendly to us," said Tom, "because we had saved the life of one of their tribe and because they knew you too."

"Yes, that was the tribe we were traveling with," said Tim. "When we told them what we wanted to do, they helped us fix up the canoe we have. Some one had punched a hole in it."

"Yah, I bunched dot hole already, I dink," admitted Fritz.

"Ye have no more sinse than ye had before," Tim said, with disgust.

"We had to destroy those canoes to keep from being pursued," Dick volunteered. "Fritz did it because I told him to."

"Sure, he would not have the sinse to do such a thing himself," asserted Tim, determined to deny any credit to the Dutchman.

"You talks, Mr. Tim," said Fritz, "but you says nothings from your mouth out."

"Let's turn in now," laughed Dick, "and we'll let you fellows fight it out tomorrow."

"Yes, I'm tired," said Tom, "and, Dick, we can swap stories tomorrow for I have lots to tell and there is a great deal we would like to hear about your trip."

CHAPTER XVI
CONCLUSION.

"Vincennes at last," shouted Tom Dare, six days after the four boys had come together. "Maybe I'm not glad we are here."

"For myself, I haf no doubt aboud id," said Fritz.

"I'm glad we've reached here within the limit of time allowed us," Dick added.

"With the whole av two days to spare," said Tim. "Faith, an' Oi think we had best be stayin' on the outside av the town till our toime is after bein' up."

"Nein," replied Fritz. "Ve'll rest in houses already yet, und not in fields, dose two days."

"They won't be lettin' you into a house, me bye," joked Tim.

The quartet had reached the clearing and were close to the walls of the fort at Vincennes by now. From many of the doorways of the houses women and children stared at them suspiciously. The men were all away in the fields and strangers in the little frontier town were quite naturally regarded with suspicion until they became known.

The boys went directly to the fort, which was held by a handful of troops recruited from the hardy frontiersmen of the section, and Dick led the way to the man on guard at the opening of the stockade.

"We want to see the commander," he said to the trooper.

"And whom might ye be?" he queried.

"We are messengers from Charleston," Dick replied, "and have some very important orders for your captain."

"Well, you young fellers stay right where ye be, and I'll go see about it."

The man sauntered off with his head turned, keeping an eye on the boys to see that they were obeying his instructions. Then he disappeared and in a minute more they saw the same man come out of one of the log huts in the enclosure and beckon to them.

The four entered and were soon in the presence of the captain of the fort.

"Well, what can we do for you?" he asked, kindly.

"We have duplicate messages for you, captain," said Dick, "which we have brought through from Charleston. They are relative to alliances it will be necessary to make with some of your Indian neighbors, and haste is imperative."

"You have certainly had a long journey," said the captain, taking the silk wrapped packages that Tom and Dick handed him. "You are the first ones through since six weeks ago. What is the news from back home? And, by the way, may I ask your name, and those of your friends?"

Dick told him their names, and also that they were connected with Captain Morgan's company.

"The Dare Boys!" ejaculated the captain. "Why, we've heard of you way out here. I am certainly glad to shake hands with such brave fighters for freedom's cause."

The boys modestly disclaimed any undue share of praise and assured the captain that there were any number of patriots, just like themselves, who did as much for the cause as they did.

"What are your plans now?" asked the captain.

"Why, just at present, I think we would all enjoy a wash and several hours' solid, undisturbed sleep."

"Nefer mind the wash," said Fritz, yawning.

The captain smiled. "I guess you can have all the rest you want right over here," he said, leading the way to another small room fitted with bunks about the walls. "You boys tumble right in here while I go over these papers you have brought, and we will call you in time for dinner to-night. That will give you a chance to get a little rest. The men will all want to see you to-night and hear your news and stories, but you won't be disturbed till then."

"That will be fine," said Dick.

"And, captain," called Tim after him, "we'll be havin' foine appetites by evening, I'm not doubtin'."

"Don't worry," replied the frontiersman, laughing. "We'll attend to that all right."

"We want to get in good shape for our trip back," said Tom. "So here goes for a good snooze."

Those of our readers who are interested in what happened to the Dare Boys and their comrades on the return trip and in their further unexpected adventures amongst the Indians of that unsettled region, can follow them in the next volume, entitled, "The Dare Boys in the Northwest."

That night the boys were given a warm welcome by the men and officers of the post. They told the amusing incidents of their adventurous trip amidst the hearty laughter of their new friends.

"You boys better stay right here and join us," one of them suggested. "We'd show you plenty of excitement."

"No, thanks," Dick replied. "I guess we better travel along towards home."

And after a two-days' rest, they did; that is, to be more accurate, they started.

CPSIA information can be obtained
at www.ICGtesting.com
Printed in the USA
LVHW110852190521
687790LV00006B/281